Slightly Slower 66

John Mulhern III

foreword by James J. O'Donnell

Copyright © 2015 by John Mulhern III.
ISBN 978-0-578-17372-6
All rights reserved.
This book may not be reproduced, in whole or in part, including illustrations, in any form (beyond that copying permitted by Sections 107 and 108 of U.S. Copyright Law and except by reviewers for the public press), without written permission from the author.

Designed by John Mulhern III
Set in Adobe Garamond Pro, Kinescope, and Minion Pro type by John Mulhern III.

To my wonderful wife Ivelis, without whom even consideration of this trip or this book would have been impossible.

Table of Contents

Author's Note, Acknowledgments, and Thanks — vii

Foreword by Jim O'Donnell — ix

Outfitting and Preparation — xi
    Considering a Third Run at the Mother Road • Choosing the Centennial • Naming *Louis*
    Making Another Trip to the Corvette Museum • Heading Home with *Louis*
    Detailed Route 66 Planning Begins • Getting *Louis* Ready for a "Big Trip"
    [Sidebar: Configuring *Louis*]

Staging: from Bryn Mawr, PA to Chicago, IL — 1
    On the Road Again • Stopping at a Museum • Cuyohoga Falls Impresses
    Another Cold Morning in Ohio • A Beautiful Spring Day in Chicago
    [Sidebar: The Corvette Generations]

Day 1: from Chicago, IL to St. Louis, MO — 5
    Here We Go! • Exiting Metropolitan Chicago • Joliet and Elwood
    Actually Stopping for the Gemini Giant • Breakfast and a Classic Gas Station in Dwight
    Change, Always Change Along the Old Route • Normal? Yes, Normal
    Lincoln, Lincoln, and More Lincoln • A Capital Building in Springfield
    In St. Louis on Our First Night

Day 2: from Chicago, IL to Springfield, MO — 13
    Louis and the Gateway Arch • Friends and Lunch in Rolla
    Heading Towards Springfield, Missouri • Our First Classic Motel Stop on the Trip
    Flame Surprises [Sidebar: Navigating the Mulhern Way in 2015]

Day 3: from Springfield, MO to Tulsa, OK — 19
    Headed Due West • A Quiet Portion of the Route • Just a Few Miles in Kansas
    Don't Miss That Bridge! • Baxter Springs • Traveling the Ribbon Road
    The Blue Whale of Catoosa • Finally Getting the Accommodations Right

Day 4: from Tulsa, OK to Tucumcari, NM — 25
    A Full Day Traveling the Mother Road • Leaving Tulsa • The Only Round Barn …
    Two Excellent Museums in Southwestern Oklahoma • Here Comes the Panhandle
    Tucumcari Tonite! • We Finally Actually Stay at the Blue Swallow
    Eating and Drinking at the Pow Wow • Night Falls in Tucumcari
    [Sidebar: Traveling Together After Twenty Years]

Day 5: from Tucumcari, NM to Santa Fe, NM — 33
    Beginning a Shorter Driving Day • Stopping in Santa Rosa
    Some Lonely and Beautiful Miles • Happily Back in Santa Fe • Geronimo Astounds, Again

Day 6: from Santa Fe, NM to Holbrook, AZ 37
    Reluctantly Leaving Santa Fe • A Truly Great Breakfast • Staying on the Pre-1937 Route
    Arizona Beckons • The Natural Awesomeness of the Petrified Forest
    A Night at the Wigwam [Sidebar: Inexact Memory When Retaking a Long Route]

Day 7: from Holbrook, AZ to Barstow, CA 43
    Another Long Day on The Road • Parking on a Corner in Winslow, Arizona
    Flagstaff and Williams • Some Great Driving in Arizona • A Beloved Diner in Kingman
    Serious Twisties Along the Sitgreaves Pass • … And Here We Are in California
    Some Route 66 Sites Saved and Some Fading Away • Bagdad and All That
    A Quiet Night in Barstow [Sidebar: A Short History of Our Cameras on Route 66]

Day 8: from Barstow, CA to Santa Monica, CA 51
    Beginning Our Final Day on Route 66 • Driving Slow Miles to the Coast
    Heading Down the Arroyo Seco • We Make It to the Finish—Again

The Return: from Santa Monica, CA to Bryn Mawr, PA 55
    A Night Aboard the Queen Mary • Turning Back East
    One of the Seven Wonders of the Industrial World
    Serious Weather and Crazy Beauty in Utah • Wonderful Denver • Straight Across Kansas
    Back in Kansas City • More Than Halfway Home • Smooth Progress on Our Last Day Out

Afterword: Thoughts on What Route 66 Means in 2015 61

Lists 63

Annotated Bibliography 65

Index 67

Credits 71

Perhaps the best car shot of the trip—*Louis* in the Painted Desert portion of the Petrified Forest National Park, New Mexico

Author's Note, Acknowledgments, and Thanks

Author's Note

When we had finished the trip detailed in this book in mid-April, my wife Ivelis informed me that she expected a book about it and would like it to be complete by no later than Thanksgiving Day 2015. With those marching orders, I got straight to work. Very few of our friends and acquaintances were surprised as it leaked out that I was once again hard at work on a travel book—many assumed that since I had written one about our Route 66 trip in 2005, I would write one about this particular trip.

My hopes were to kick it up a notch from the last two books I have published, so I have worked harder on both form and content. In a way, this book completes a sort of trilogy of one book each on three cross-country trips in three different Corvettes.

I wanted this book to work both for Corvette people and for people who know nothing or next to nothing about Corvettes. So, there are explanations of some Corvette things that many Corvette people may find more than a bit basic and that some non-Corvette people may find far too extensive. I hope the reader will forgive this inability to leave any supposedly needed detail out.

Acknowledgments and Thanks

First, thanks to my wife Ivelis, for her assistance, support, understanding, and most of all, her great love.

A very grateful thank you to Jim O'Donnell for agreeing to write what turned out to be an amazing foreword under considerable time pressure.

Thanks to Lisa Campeau for her copyediting assistance. Any slip-ups in the text that missed her eagle eye are my responsibility alone.

Thanks to Greg Carson, Matt Edmonds, and Allyson Fredeen for assistance in securing the rights to images and photographs. Thanks also to Cathie Stevanovich, Jason Trumpy, Jennifer Yuan, and the members of Corvette Guru for fact-checking assistance. In addition, thanks to Michael Heath for digital photography advice.

Finally, thanks to Paul McCartney for "Driving Rain," the inspirational song for this book. Listening to Paul sing about a drive up the Pacific Coast Highway in his Corvette convertible always makes me want to get back on the road.

Foreward

It's hard to find the west any more. Frederick Jackson Turner, who had taught at Wisconsin, was sitting at Harvard when he declared the frontier closed in an influential book in 1920, but Buffalo Bill had started turning the west into a theme park as early as the 1880s. Owen Wister's *The Virginian* had canonized the western yarn in 1902 and Gary Cooper embalmed it in the early talking movie of 1929.

But you can find other dates and from where I sit I'll point to November 17, 1961, when Jack Kennedy and Lyndon Johnson came to Phoenix to celebrate the life and career of the still-flourishing Carl Hayden, Arizona's first congressman, to make sure he won re-election one more time in 1962. Jet airplanes had found Phoenix a couple of years earlier and the Interstate Highway System was creeping across that west. (Hayden was instrumental in the 1930s in passing a bill that made sure that federal highway funds were distributed on the basis of square miles, not population—a critical choice in making sure that the still-empty western regions would be served.)

In that range of time comes the short happy life of the original US highway system. The federal highways got their familiar numbers (odd numbers north/south, even east/west, starting from the northeast and US 1 in Maine and ending with 101 in California) only in 1926. The first stretch of officially-recognized Interstate highway opened in Kansas in 1956. In between, it's good to mark the Pennsylvania Turnpike's opening in 1940 as the first controlled-access highway of the future.

But that short life was revolutionary. It made possible an American unity and mobility that had been much more notional and hypothetical before that. I'll give you two benchmarks. Steinbeck's *Grapes of Wrath* was published in 1939, capturing the experience of the poorest of the poor at one of the worst moments in American history: and it's a novel about those US highways. Even ten years earlier, getting a car and heading for California would have been flat out impossible for those people. Second, in 1941, my father, then a postal clerk in Holyoke, MA, had saved up for a Chevy and headed out with two "girl cousins" (chaperoning each other I doubt not) for a

Jim definitely travels—with Gary the koala in Brisbane

grand circular drive that took him to Yellowstone and San Francisco and Yosemite and the Grand Canyon and even then to O'Donnell, Texas. (I followed him there 40-odd years later.) His photos of the Golden Gate Bridge and the Hoover Dam are important because those were the high-tech triumphs of American can-do spirit in those end-of-depression days, markers of what was to come.

Of all those roads of that short golden age, Route 66 lingers longest. Oh, sure, you see Lincoln Highway signs here and there across the country and it's fun to find the exact street corner in San Francisco where it ends, but nobody wrote songs about the Lincoln Highway. The song dates to 1946, first recorded by Nat King Cole, and the TV series to 1960. The road was decommissioned in 1985.

And then began its afterlife. It's a shrine to a moment of American venture, confidence, and inclusiveness. When Ivelis and John Mulhern start packing the storage compartment on *Louis* for their great journey, they are more or less consciously reproducing the packing of covered wagons and stage coaches and jitney busses and Model T's that made these runs long before. I like the fact that their journey starts in Kentucky when they pick up *Louis* for his first spin. Kentucky is Daniel Boone country and if anyone represents both the historical and the remembered drive west, it's old Dan'l, born in Birdsboro PA, a few miles from the Mulhern home, and died in aptly-named Defiance MO (they passed a few miles south of there coming out of Saint Louis).

We all get confused and muddled about that west

of ours and sometimes we're as confused as the protagonists of Luis Buñuel's film *The Milky Way* about just what century we're living in. But it's good that there are these zones of confusion and memory and respect for our elders. The journey of *Louis* is a far sight easier than what old Dan'l or Tom Joad knew, but in many important respects it's still the same journey.

And that—quite apart from the easy affability of John and Ivelis that comes through here—is why reading this book will make you smile.

Jim O'Donnell
Tempe AZ

Outfitting and Preparation

Considering a Third Run at the Mother Road

At least basic preparation for our April 2015 Route 66 trip began shortly after the completion of our April 2005 trip. That trip, detailed in *A 21st Century Road Trip* (J3Studio Press, 2006), was immensely satisfying, but time constraints also made us extremely aware of where and when we simply could not stop. We resolved to change this as much as possible the next time, so our code name for whenever we would drive Route 66 again became first *Route 66 Slow* and than (at Ivelis' suggestion) *Slow 66*.

Real life intruded over the next several years. We had tentative plans for traveling Route 66 in spring 2010, but that timing just didn't work out. At that point, we decided to put the trip off for another five years—April 2015 would be our twentieth wedding anniversary.

Choosing the Centennial

In mid 2011, Ivelis and I got a chance to see the two prototypes for the 2012 Centennial Edition Corvettes at the absolutely amazing (if you are remotely interested in *either* cars or industrial design you should go if you ever get a chance) **General Motors Heritage Center** in Sterling Heights, Michigan. When Ivelis sees a Corvette of any age that she *really* likes she a) stops talking and b) her knees knock. This happened with the two prototype Centennials, but I wasn't sure how limited their availability was, so I made no promises. I did, however, make a mental note to investigate further.

On a Saturday morning in early August of that same year we were talking about Corvettes over lunch just after having run a 5K together. I looked across at Ivelis and reminded her that she had always talked about having Corvette as her daily driver—the car she would drive most of the year. "If not now, when?" I pointed out. Ivelis now tells almost everybody who asks about story of the purchase decision that I caught her in a "moment of weakness" but I believe that it was quite simply the right time.

Later on that same day, I sent a request for a quote to a range of Chevrolet dealers, some local to us and some national. My first response (only a couple of hours later) was from a dealer in Montana, but I didn't care about the distance—we had already decided that we would pick up the car at the **National Corvette Museum** in Bowling Green, Kentucky. We actually ended ordering the car from that very responsive dealer in Montana, doing it all over email, fax, and FedEx.

Naming Louis

It's an Ivelis and John "thing;" we name all our cars, but this particular one was named far more quickly than any of our other cars. Louis Chevrolet, a Swiss-born racecar driver of French descent, founded Chevrolet in 1911. Every Centennial Edition that was made for the 2012 model year has no less than *seven* pictures of Louis Chevrolet

One of the two Centennial Edition prototypes we saw

Centennial logo on the sail panels

with his distinctive racer's cap, goggles, and mustache on it: one on each of the four wheel center caps, one on each sail panel behind the side windows, and one on the steering wheel. So, Ivelis and I had agreed that our Centennial was going to be named *Louis* before we actually took delivery.

Over the next two months, we watched our car's build status move steadily forward in GM's relatively primitive but reasonably effective on-line tracking system. *Louis* was actually built late in September in Bowling Green, where all Corvettes have been built since the middle of the 1981 model year.

Making Another Trip to the Corvette Museum

On the afternoon of October 12th, 2011, we flew from Philadelphia to Nashville, with a relatively short layover in Atlanta. With the assistance of the delivery team at the Corvette Museum, we rented a Chevrolet Malibu (at least it was a Chevrolet) at the Nashville airport and drove for about 67 miles along first Interstate 40 and then Interstate 65 on our way north to Bowling Green. That night, we stayed at a Hampton Inn on Three Springs Road in Bowling Green that lists proximity to the National Corvette Museum as one of its primary selling points.

We woke up early the next morning and drove just a few miles to the museum. After signing some paperwork, we were taken on a relaxed and personalized tour of the museum—the actual plant was unexpectedly closed so we had to take a rain check on that interesting part of the experience. When the tour was finished, we went to the delivery section of the museum, where we went through the actual vehicle

A *very* happy couple outside the Corvette Museum

Configuring Louis

One enduring (perhaps endearing?) rule in the Mulhern III household is that Ivelis picks the basics of our new cars—it is then my job to make sure we have the correct specific configuration.

Louis was going to be a daily driver, so we quickly decided that he would be what Chevrolet calls a "base coupe"—the bottom of the Corvette line in 2012. There were a couple of the reasons for this choice, but the primary one was the availability of more all-season tire options—important in a car that would be driven year 'round in a temperate climate. *Louis* would also be a "narrow-body"—about three inches thinner and a little shorter than the Grand Sport, Z06, and ZR1 versions of the 2012 Corvette.

Every Corvette made in 2012 included a "small block" V8 engine, antilock disc brakes, active handling, traction control, keyless access with push button start, dual-zone air conditioning, power steering, cruise control, and power seats.

Since we had decided on a Centennial Edition (RPO **ZLC**), a good portion of our additional equipment was already picked out for us, including Carbon Flash Metallic paint (as Ivelis says, a very "sparkly" black), black red-line wheels with red brake calipers (**J6F**), the aforementioned Louis Chevrolet insignia, matte black racing stripes (crazy!), and special front badging. Inside, the interior is a comfortable black micro fiber suede with red piping.

All Centennials also required at least a **3LT** interior, which included power-telescoping steering column, memory package, heated sport seats, and a nine speaker stereo. Mechanically, all Centennials include the wonderful Magnetic Select Ride (**F55**).

I added the Dual Mode Exhaust System (**NPP**), the Six-speed Paddle Shift Automatic Transmission (**MYC**), the Dual Roof Package (**C2L**), and the Battery Protection Package (**BPP**). Finally, we added Corvette Museum Delivery (**R8C**), which we had done once before back in 2003.

delivery process with our enthusiastic delivery team member. Following that, Ivelis drove *Louis* outside very carefully, a few more pictures were taken in the front of the museum, and we were on our way.

Heading Home with Louis

Of course we took the scenic route home from Bowling Green, stopping for very celebratory nights in Knoxville and Richmond and driving a total of about 930 miles in two and a half days. Very early on, we realized that *Louis* was an exceptionally comfortable long distance driver—after driving most of the 450 miles between Knoxville and Richmond on our second day in the car, I got out at our hotel stop for the night feeling I could have driven for many hours more.

In front of our Japanese maple in November 2011

got to make the call because the car was going to be her driver. She wanted "LOVE," but that was taken in every state I checked. "LUFF" was, surprisingly, available in Pennsylvania, so we ordered it and had it on the car by late November 2015.

Detailed Route 66 Planning Begins

With the vehicle for our next Route 66 trip chosen and in hand, I began to do more detailed planning—there would likely be few wonderful or unexpected experiences along the route if I didn't get the baseline preparations correct.

A scenic stop on the way home from Kentucky

Once we returned home, Ivelis settled quite happily into having a new Corvette as a daily driver (tough duty!). Winter was coming quickly, so one of the first items on my agenda was to order all-season tires from the wonderful and competent folks at TireRack—*Louis* had shipped with Goodyear Eagle F1 GS-2 ultra high performance summer tires that would be less than useful once the temperature dropped below 45 degrees. As I drove home from getting our all-season Michelin Pilot Sport ZPs mounted and balanced on October 31st, both of us actually saw the beginning of a very early winter snowfall.

Next came choosing a vanity license plate—Ivelis

Louis posing for our 2011 holiday card

The first important question was how many days we would have for the trip, as both of us work full time—there are some Route 66 devotees that believe it can't possibly be done correctly in less than a month or so. In the end, we were able to allot eight days for Route 66, instead of our previous six (in 2005) and five (in 2000). With this extra time, we would be traveling an average of a little less than 300 miles a day while actually on the Mother Road. In our modern and comfortable car, that low mileage requirement would mean we could stop almost anywhere along the route if either of us was remotely interested.

Our philosophy on this trip was to travel as much of the old road as possible, but not to get crazy about it. If something was closed, inaccessible, or "no trespassing," we would simply move on and we would also try not to get *too* perturbed if we missed a turn or two.

Timing was also important: we would definitely want to both leave the Chicago metropolitan area and enter the Los Angeles metropolitan area on a weekend to avoid at least some of the traffic craziness. Thus, we were looking at Saturday through Saturday or Sunday through Sunday for the actual Route 66 portion of our trip. After much consideration and a couple of false starts with planning, we ended up deciding on a Sunday start from Chicago because it was a better fit for our overall plans.

With the basic bones of the Route 66 portion of the trip in place, I worked on the before and after. Our previous experience told us that we would be able to comfortably stage from our house to Chicago in two days. Our return trip from the California coast would require more *alacrity* (as Al Michaels says)—I allotted six days, but believed we could likely do it in five *full* driving days.

Getting Louis Ready for a "Big Trip"

The two of us had done cross-country trips with cars notably less capable than *Louis*, so we felt that we had at least somewhat of a handle on preparing for this trip. We also took some multi-day trips in the car, including a Lake Erie trip in April 2012, a "Southern Gallivant" in July 2012, and a birthday visit to the absolutely stunning (you should go!) **Auburn Cord Duesenberg Automobile Museum** in Auburn, Indiana in May 2013.

My first preparatory task was to carefully verify that the luggage we expected to bring would fit along with all our other supplies—don't make that rookie mistake!

For Christmas 2013, my sister Helen, her husband Michael, and their car-crazy little boy Julian purchased us some add-on cup holders—*Louis'* stock cup holders (though better than those in any previous Corvette generation) are not that impressive. Having somewhere to put our coffee is essential for these long road trips.

Ivelis with her beloved *Louis* in front of a covered bridge in October 2014

As we always do for long trips in any of our cars, *Louis* would carry a Halon fire extinguisher in a quick disconnect mount attached to the fore-and-aft adjustment rails under the passenger seat.

Since *Louis* is a daily driver, he rides on Michelin Pilot Sport all-season run-flat tires from mid-fall to mid-spring. Based on experience gained traveling about two thirds of the same route at the same time of the year in 2005 (we saw snow twice), we decided to keep the all-seasons on for the trip rather than switching to the stock summer tires.

Staging: from Bryn Mawr, PA to Chicago, IL

On the Road Again

Ivelis and I both woke up quite excited on the morning of Friday, April 3rd. After packing *Louis'* rear storage area pretty darn full with luggage, supplies, and tools, we left Bryn Mawr at about 8:00 AM in the morning with the temperature hovering around 60 degrees.

Entering Ohio—once again in heavy rain

Packed full and ready to go

There was little driving glamour planned for this first day—we were just looking to get well into Ohio at a reasonable time of day and in one piece. We got on the Pennsylvania Turnpike in King of Prussia and pointed *Louis* west along it for a little over 340 miles through some rather *questionable* rain—Ivelis reminds me that we've seen discouraging weather in Pennsylvania and Ohio at the beginning of all three of our Route 66 trips.

There's always some adjustment, that first day on the road on one of our long trips. There are changes in what we've packed, what traveling aids we have, and sometimes what car we are driving. Ivelis drove on as I futzed with our electronics and various other variables.

As we neared Pittsburgh, we stayed on the Turnpike as it curved northwest. We continued to drive on through bands of moderate to heavy rain. About four miles after crossing into Ohio, we fueled *Louis* at the Sunoco in the Mahoning Valley service plaza before heading north along first Interstate 680 and then 422 towards the city of Warren.

Stopping at a Museum

Our first stop of any note on this trip was at the **National Packard Museum** on Mahoning Avenue in Warren. To borrow from the AAA travel guide usage, this museum is a "gem"—really nice people, cool exhibits, and a large and distinctively Packard radiator grill as the quietly clever main entrance.

Clever Packard museum entrance

All of the museum's exhibits were good, but I particularly enjoyed their multiple Packard Caribbeans from the mid-1950s—a *major* weakness of mine with their handsome lines and *tri*-tone exteriors (for when two-tone just isn't enough). We lingered at the museum for quite a while, but decided at some point that we needed to move on to our stopping place for the night.

Packard tri-tone: Dover White, Scottish Heather, Maltese Gray

From Warren, we headed west on Interstate 80 for several miles. Near Boston Heights, we turned south on Ohio 8 towards Cuyahoga Falls.

Cuyahoga Falls Impresses

We stayed for the night at the **Sheraton Suites Akron Cuyahoga Falls**, which, as you might expect, is located right next to the rather gorgeous falls. After settling into our comfortable "creek view" room, we had an enjoyable and *huge* meal at the very scenic **Beau's on the River** in the hotel—don't go to Beau's if you aren't hungry!

After our dinner, we met a longtime virtual Corvette friend of ours named Ken for the first time in the physical world—he lives just a few blocks from the hotel. The three of us had a few quiet but happy drinks at the hotel bar as we finished our first day on the road.

Another Cold Morning in Ohio

The next morning, we woke, dressed, packed, and checked out of our pleasant Sheraton. When we walked out to the hotel parking lot at about 9:30 AM on a brisk Saturday morning, we found *Louis* covered in frost—it had dropped a few degrees below freezing overnight.

I stabbed at my remote to open the rear hatch, but nothing happened. "No problem," said Ivelis, as I stood behind the car wondering what to do. She quickly opened the driver's side door, crawled into the back, and forcefully popped the hatch from the inside. Both of us packed the car, cleared the frost off

The Corvette Generations

The various Corvette generations are often designated by C1 through C7, though this is a relatively recent practice—the Corvette cognoscenti previously identified generations differently. The generations are generally agreed to be:

C1 (1953-1962)—the first Corvettes, often called "solid-axles" because they're the only Corvettes without an independent rear suspension. These Corvettes changed vastly between 1953 and 1962, gaining a much-needed V8 in 1955, and both fuel injection and four-speed manual transmissions in 1957

C2 (1963-1967)—a complete redesign, the Sting Rays, also called "mid-years," these were the first Corvettes with independent rear suspension, hidden headlights, and (in 1965) four-wheel disk brakes. In 2004, *Automobile* magazine called the 1967 Sting Ray the "coolest car in history"

C3 (1968-1982)—often called "sharks," these were initially derided as merely a styling change but ended up much loved, getting the Corvette through the tenuous and low-performance mid-1970s and modernization in the late 1970s and early 1980s

C4 (1984-1996)—a long overdue complete redesign from the "sharks," these were arguably the first modern Corvettes, being the first Corvettes to have rack and pinion steering, anti-lock brakes, six-speed manual transmissions, traction control, and air bags

C5 (1997-2004)—another complete redesign, designed from the ground up to yield exotic car performance in an easy-to-maintain package

C6 (2005-2013)—not a complete redesign like the C4 or C5, but full of useful enhancements and refinements, these cars changed significantly over their tenure, gaining new engines, transmissions, seats, and electronics

C7 (2014-?)—the absolute latest Corvettes are a substantial redesign and the fastest stock versions ever

Louis covered in frost in Cuyahoga Falls

the windows, and were soon on our way.

We headed north from Cuyahoga Falls along Ohio 8 until we joined Interstate 80 again and headed west, joining Interstate 90 near Elyria and crossing into Indiana near Metz. At about 1:30 PM, we stopped for lunch at the Elkhart rest stop—a stop that has more than a little bit of 1960s style. After lunch, we filled *Louis* up with some more premium fuel and got back on the Indiana Toll Road.

A little further along the interstate, we drove by the **TireRack** corporate headquarters (with test track) and distribution center clearly visible to our left in South Bend. They have been providers of *many* sets of tires (including the excellent Michelin Pilot Sports that we were using on this trip) to us over the years, along with various other tire and wheel related accessories. I always find it interesting to see distribution centers of products we use—you know these goods are coming from somewhere, but you never think you might actually see that location.

After passing South Bend, we continued along Interstate 80/90 for about 70 miles toward the Illinois border, splitting away from Interstate 80 in Gary as we headed for Chicago.

A Beautiful Spring Day in Chicago

We entered Chicago along the Chicago Skyway toll bridge and road, which was built in 1958, for about eight miles before joining Interstate 94 for another five miles.

Heading onto the Chicago Skyway

Once we exited downtown onto the Lake Shore Drive and continue onto Columbus Drive, actually getting to our hotel proved to be a somewhat painful comedy of errors—half the streets seemed to be closed and/or under construction. This confused our GPS, which confused me (I was navigating) and I passed this confusion on to Ivelis (who was driving). After about three or four extra miles of making what Ivelis calls "crop circles", we finally made it to our hotel's parking garage at about 2:30 PM Central time.

Overhead view of the TireRack headquarters in South Bend

Our hotel in better times

In Chicago, we stayed at **The Congress Plaza Hotel**, an older (portions date from 1893) hotel that has definitely seen better times. It is, however, reasonably priced, in a great location, and our room had an excellent view of the magnificent Grant Park, which is on the National Register of Historic Places. After getting quickly settled in our room, we headed out to **Grant Park** and Lake Michigan.

Made from Cadillac parts—flower sculptures in Chicago's Grant Park

The previous day's sketchy weather had cleared—it was a lovely early spring day in Chicago. We spent a few hours in the park, first walking straight to the shore of Lake Michigan along Congress Parkway and past the Buckingham Fountain (not yet flowing as of early April). We then turned north along the Lakefront Trail and walked up to Dusable Harbor and the Columbia Yacht Club's very handsome *MV Abegweit* ice-breaking ferry, commissioned in 1947.

The *MV Abegweit* on the Chicago lake shore

On our walk back to the hotel, we stopped for a few minutes while I took pictures of some gorgeous flower sculptures in the South President's Court portion of Grant Park. These, titled *Lilies*, were created by Chicago artist Dessa Kirk from old Cadillac parts, and thus some meaningful Route 66 foreshadowing for us—I love when things tie together.

After changing for dinner, we walked north along Michigan Avenue for a little over a mile before taking a left on Ohio Avenue and a right on Rush Street. We arrived just a little early for our reservations at **David Burke's Prime House**, where we had—as Ivelis had told me to expect—a really excellent dinner, with Ivelis ordering her beloved Silver Oak Alexander Valley cabernet sauvignon by the glass. Afterwards, we walked slowly back along Michigan Avenue to The Congress Plaza, had a nightcap at The Congress Lounge, and turned in for the night, excited to start our Route 66 portion of the trip in the morning.

Road Trip Statistics

Travel time for staging: **2 days**
Miles travelled on this leg: **785**
Total travel time: **2 days**
Total miles traveled: **785**
Miles from home at the end of this leg (shortest reasonable route): 748

Day 1: from Chicago, IL to St. Louis, MO

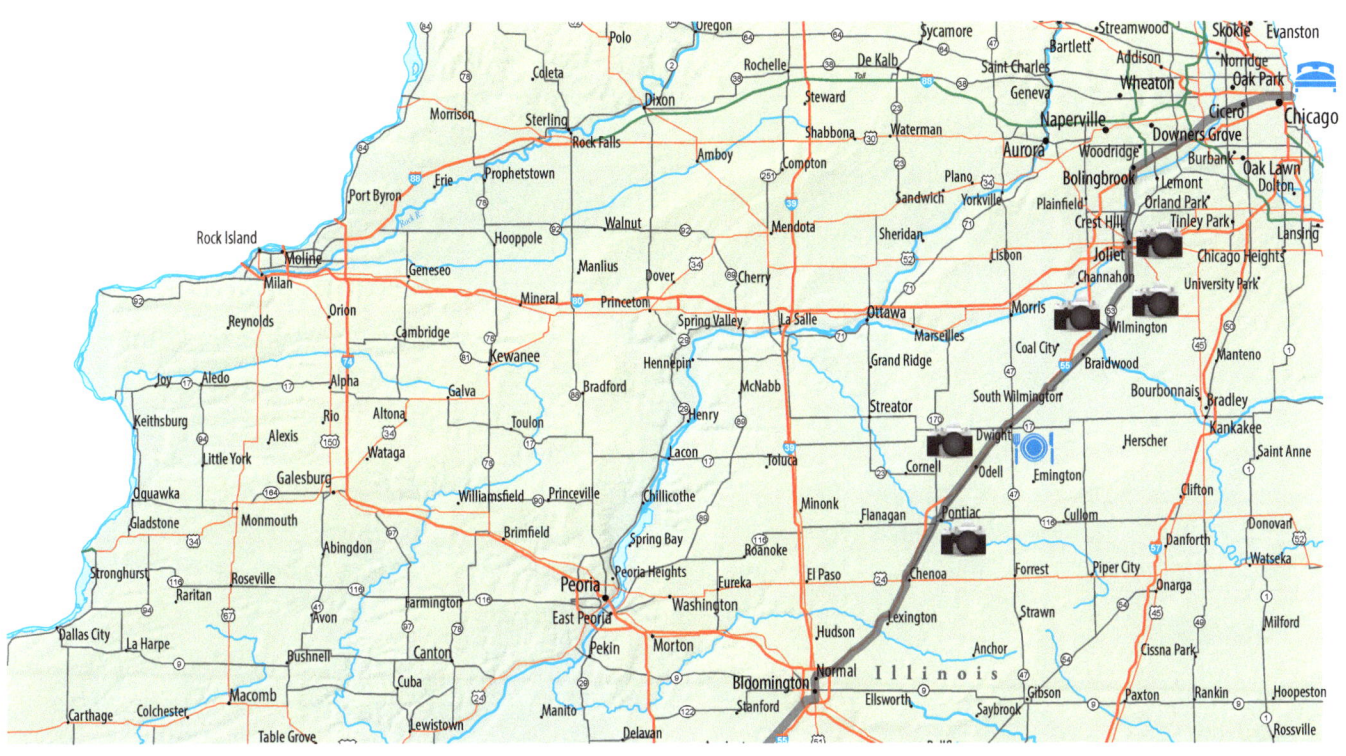

The morning drive from Chicago to Bloomington

Here We Go!

On Easter morning, we woke up reasonably early, showered, dressed, packed, and checked out of The Congress Plaza. Once we had walked outside for a few hundred feet to the hotel's affiliated parking garage, we didn't have to wait at all for the valet to bring our car—I noticed fairly quickly that Ivelis' handsome *Louis* was parked rather conspicuously right out front.

My biggest concern on the morning of our first day actually on Route 66 itself was getting out of the Chicago metropolitan area reasonably quickly. At about 8:30 AM, we successfully picked up the eastern beginning of the Mother Road at the intersection of Michigan Avenue and Adams Street and headed due west on Adams for a good bit longer than I remembered from previous trips (it is actually a little over two miles) before taking an angled left onto Ogden Avenue.

Route 66 begins on Adams Street

Exiting Metropolitan Chicago

I definitely felt that we were making good progress as we drove along on Ogden Avenue (named for Chicago's first mayor—William B. Ogden) in fairly light traffic for almost eight miles through Cicero and Berwyn. We made a left onto Harlem Avenue followed by a fairly quick right onto Joliet Road as we passed through Lyons.

A little bit further down the road in the village of McCook, we detoured right on 55th Street and left on East Avenue before rejoining Joliet Road—over the years a rock quarry carelessly (recklessly?) dug *much* too close to the old route.

Our surroundings began to look a lot less urban

and a lot more suburban as we drove the next few miles through Countryside and Indian Head Park. Just as I had gotten reasonably comfortable with these changes, we reached our first point where old 66 simply *vanishes* and you must get on the interstate—in this case, we got on Interstate 55 South (it was too early in the day to stop at **Dell Rhea's Chicken Basket** in Willowbrook).

Joliet and Elwood

We stayed on Interstate 55 for about eight miles before exiting back onto Joliet Road near Romeoville. In Romeoville, we joined Highway 53 for about ten miles before heading into Joliet itself. In Joliet, we stopped for some quite silly pictures at **Dick's Towing** before heading on toward Elwood.

Posing with an old police car outside Dick's Towing in Joliet

The village of Elwood is likely the inspiration for how Elwood Blues of *The Blues Brothers* got his first name. As we drove along Highway 53 in Joliet and Elwood, we saw many signs of the famous duo, including a statue of the two brothers dancing on top of the **Rich & Creamy** ice cream parlor (there's a picture in the Lists section located in the back of this book) and a "Bluesmobile" (a 1974 Dodge Monaco sedan with a huge siren on the roof) mounted on a pole at the **Route 66 Food N Fuel**. Shortly thereafter, NASCAR's **Chicagoland Speedway** 1.5-mile tri-oval was a notable sight on our left as we continued to drive southwest along Highway 53.

Being on the road far from home on Easter was a little different for us and probably accounted for our decision to stop a little further down the road at the **Abraham Lincoln National Cemetery** just south of Elwood. The cemetery is relatively new: it was dedicated in 1999 and its 982 acres were formerly the location of the Joliet Arsenal, active from 1941 to the mid-1970s.

I parked, Ivelis and I got out of the car, and we held hands as we quietly viewed the cemetery from the memorial walk on what was a beautiful morning. Thinking of all the sacrifice visible on those almost endless tombstones (there will eventually be *400,000* burial spaces at the cemetery) and more than a little chastened, we got returned to the road and headed towards Wilmington.

Actually Stopping for the Gemini Giant

After driving right on by the famous **Gemini Giant** in Wilmington two times previously, we finally stopped just north of the center of town for some pictures next to the big green guy. Despite the **Launching Pad Drive-In** where the statue is located

Bluesmobile with correct siren in Joliet

Louis dwarfed by the Gemini Giant in Wilmington

having been closed for several years now, *somebody* is definitely maintaining the circa 1965 "muffler man"—he isn't in perfect shape, but he's definitely not fading away ...

When we had finished visiting with the giant, we continued along Highway 53 for about five miles to Braidwood, where we passed the circa 1956 **Polk-a-Dot Drive In** with its various Elvi and various spellings (one of them is in the photograph Ivelis took below).

Appropriate lighting in Dwight

Elvis plays outside the Polk-A-Dot in Braidwood

After Braidwood, it was another seven miles through Godley, Braceville, and Mazonia before heading into the village of Gardner. Until relatively recently, Gardner was home to the **Riviera Roadhouse**, which was said to have been a favorite haunt of Al Capone—it burned down in June 2010. After passing through Gardner, we followed the Frontage Road (we would once again get *quite* used to that descriptor!) for about seven miles as we headed to the village of Dwight.

Breakfast and a Classic Gas Station in Dwight

Upon entering Dwight, we turned left onto Highway 47 and right onto Waupansie Street. At about 11:00 AM, we stopped for a late breakfast at the **Old Route 66 Family Restaurant**, which was suggested by more than one of our various Route 66 travel guides. When we entered, I was forced to admit to the hostess that we had neglected to make reservations on this Easter morning—something I had not considered in my fairly extensive planning (I always miss *something* on these trips). She still managed to

seat us in a nice Route 66-themed booth where we had a good and filling meal.

After we finished eating, both of us took a bunch of beauty shots at the restored circa 1933 **Ambler's Texaco** gas station located just across the street and on the National Register of Historic Places. The station is named after manager Basil "Tubby" Ambler, who operated it for almost thirty years from 1938 to 1966; it now serves as Dwight's visitor's center.

Restored Ambler's Texaco station in Dwight

Change, Always Change Along the Old Route

In a notable change from what we saw ten years ago, there are no longer wires hanging from the old telephone poles along Route 66 in Illinois. The copper in them has gotten far more expensive over the last decade, so it was fairly suddenly worth recovering—and the wires have now completely vanished, significantly changing at least one aspect of heading down that part of the old road.

It was definitely turning out to be an old gas station

Beautifully restored Standard Oil station in Odell

Mural celebrates an old candy store

kind of the day. About six miles further down the Frontage Road, we took a left onto West Street and stopped at an absolutely gorgeous **Standard Oil** gas station in Odell. Built in 1932 and *beautifully* restored by dedicated volunteers from the Route 66 Association of Illinois beginning in 1999, it is, of course, on the National Register of Historic Places. On this bright April morning, I think it was looking its blue and white best.

After our stop, we returned to the Frontage Road. About eight miles further along in the small and pretty city of Pontiac, we managed to get temporarily lost for the first (but *definitely* not the last) time on this trip—we ended up following the Route 66 markers northeast instead of southwest a few times. We made a few of what Ivelis politely calls "crop circles" and traveled a couple of unnecessary miles before eventually figuring things out and heading back in the correct direction.

The two of us would have almost certainly taken

On the Mother Road between Pontiac and Normal, driving south

The afternoon drive from Bloomington to St. Louis

the time to stop at the highly recommended **Route 66 Association of Illinois Hall of Fame and Museum** in Pontiac, but it is closed on Easter Sunday every year.

Normal? Yes, Normal

Ivelis and I drove on, following the Route 66 route on the Frontage Road (is it worthy of capital letters?) through Chenoa, Lexington, and Towanda for a little over thirty miles on our way towards the large town of Normal. Normal was named after what was Illinois State Normal ("normal" was a designation for a teacher's college in the 1800s) University and is now simply Illinois State University. We turned left on Henry Street that turns into Pine Street as it curves right. After passing the circa 1931 **Sprague's Super Service**, we took another left onto Linden Street and another right on Willow Street before joining Business US 51.

Normal and the city of Bloomington are essentially co-joined, with Bloomington due south of Normal and connected to it by Business US 51. After exiting Bloomington (the world headquarters of State Farm insurance), we resumed our southwest direction, joining Veterans Parkway for a little over a mile before turning right onto Fox Creek and left onto the (you guessed it) Frontage Road. We drove along for about 12 miles through Shirley and Funks Grove (known for the Funks family's "pure maple sirup") to the village of McLean.

In McLean, we curved right on Carlisle Street and left on Main Street before taking an angled right onto US 136. We

Downey Building in Atlanta

continued along US 136 for about four miles before entering the tiny city of Atlanta, turning right and then curving left on Northeast Arch Street. Northeast Arch turned into Southeast Arch in the middle of town as we passed the handsome circa 1867 **Downey Building** (now partially occupied by the **Palms Grill Cafe**). Shortly thereafter we turned right and rejoined the Frontage Road for another six miles.

Lincoln, Lincoln, and More Lincoln

We traveled the Lincoln Parkway for a little over a mile as we headed into the city of (natch!) Lincoln. Lincoln is the only town in the United States that was named for Abraham Lincoln *before* he became president. We turned left onto Kickapoo Street, right onto Keokuk Street, and left onto Logan Street. We took an angle right onto 5th Street and a left onto Washington Street. Washington Street turned into Stringer Avenue as we crossed some more train tracks (train tracks and Route 66 are often closely paired) and took a left to rejoin the Lincoln Parkway for another two miles.

After Lincoln, we were back onto the Frontage Road for a little over 13 miles through Broadwell and Elkhart on the way to the village of Williamsville. We entered Williamsville on Oak Street and stopped for gas before we were once again forced back on Interstate 55 for about four miles. We exited onto Business Loop 55 just north of Sherman and followed it for almost five miles into the city of Springfield (birthplace of musician Morris Day).

A Capital Building in Springfield

In downtown Springfield, we stopped to take some pictures of the very impressive **Illinois State Capital** building, built over a period of 20 years beginning in 1869 at a cost of $4.5 million dollars and, of course, on the National Register of Historic Places.

After we left the capital building, we continued along Business Loop 55 until it joined Interstate 55, which we drove along for about four miles before exiting back onto the old road.

We headed almost due south (we had decided to take the post-1930 route) through Glenarm, Divernon, Farmersville, and Waggoner, continuing to jump on and off Interstate 55 when we needed to. Near the small city of Litchfield (home to the **Sky View Drive-In Theater**—in continuous operation since 1951), we began to travel more southwest again, through the tiny city of Mount Olive and the village of Hamel.

In St. Louis on Our First Night

As we closed in on St. Louis, we transferred guidance from our various Route 66 guidebooks to the TomTom GPS app on Ivelis' iPhone—our stop for the night was not on any of the old 66 routes and traffic was also beginning to get quite busy as folks returned from their Easter-related family gatherings.

Interstate 55 joins Interstate 70 and US 40 for several miles. In East St. Louis, we took exit 2C and drove across the mighty Mississippi River on the Martin Luther King Memorial Bridge—the **Chain Of Rocks Bridge** built in 1929 that was originally part of Route 66 now carries only pedestrian and bicycle traffic.

I believe that the city of St. Louis has much to recommend it, but, other than the justifiably famous **Ted Drewes' Frozen Custard**, very few vestiges of the Mother Road remain. The King Brothers Motel, the 66 Auto Court, and the especially gorgeous **Coral Court** motel are all long gone (a small portion of the circa 1941 Coral Court survives as part of an exhibit at the **Museum of Transportation** in Kirkwood). If the two of us ever travel Route 66 again (perhaps in 2025?), I don't think we'll stay in St. Louis—it almost feels like we're cheating on our travels of the Mother

Illinois State Capital building on a beautiful day

Pictures are *almost* all that is left of the Coral Court

Road.

That night we stayed at a perfectly nice modern hotel in downtown St. Louis and walked a few blocks to a perfectly nice chain steakhouse for dinner. After dinner, we headed back to our hotel. For the two of us, it had been a successful and fun first day on the Mother Road.

Road Trip Statistics

Miles traveled on our first Route 66 day: **309**
Total travel time: **3 days**
Total miles traveled to this point: **1,097**
Miles from home at the end of this leg (shortest reasonable route): **873**

Day 2: from St Louis, MO to Springfield, MO

Louis and the Gateway Arch

Ivelis and I got up, showered, dressed, had a good breakfast at our modern hotel, packed quickly, and checked out. We had decided the evening before that prior to leaving St. Louis we would at least attempt to take a picture of *Louis* and the always-spectacular **Gateway Arch**. A couple of blocks away from the hotel, I jumped out of the car with my Nikon and positioned myself across the street from the Arch grounds on the steps of the **Old Courthouse** (it deserves its name—circa 1839) as Ivelis drove around the block a few times. Despite the ongoing multi-year construction that is described as the "Gateway Arch Grounds Project," I did manage to get a few at least somewhat reclaimable pictures.

Afterwards, we headed west-southwest along Interstate 44 for several miles, passing the **Missouri Route 66 State Park** that we've stopped at twice before. Just west of the small city of Pacific, we picked up old 66, headed through Gray Summit and passed the recently closed (it managed to remain open for about 70

Ivelis and *Louis* driving in front of the Gateway Arch

The Gardenway Motel in Gray Summit recently closed

years) **Gardenway Motel** on Highway 100. In Villa Ridge, we passed the **Sunset Motel**, with its unusual sign.

There's no way of sugarcoating it—it was a cloudy, gray, and dreary day. We continued along Highway AT (crazy Missouri road names!) for five miles before joining the North Outer Road for another five miles. We crossed to the South Outer Road

Sunset Motel sign in Villa Ridge

(so descriptive!) and headed into the tiny city of Saint Clair—once known as Traveler's Repose and noted for its twin water towers, one labeled "Hot" and the other labeled "Cold." In Saint Clair, we continued along Commercial Avenue before turning on right on North Highway 30 and left on the North Outer Road.

Saint Clair's hot and cold water towers

We headed through Stanton and switched to the South Outer Road, driving almost six miles on through the small city of Sullivan, where we took a few wrong turns before figuring things out. South Outer Road turned into Springfield Road and back into South Outer Road as we headed toward the village of St. Cloud.

Old Highway 66 became South Outer Road again through Bourbon (*not* the first Bourbon we have driven through) on our way for the 11 miles to the tiny city of Cuba. In Cuba (the "Mural City") we followed Washington Street past the inviting **Wagon Wheel Motel** (built in 1935). Washington Street turned into Highway ZZ on our way to Fanning.

One of many murals in Cuba

Of course we had to stop for the **world's largest rocking chair** in tiny Fanning. The chair is 42 feet and 1 inch tall, weighs *about* 14 tons (no one is quite sure of the exact weight), and was built in 2008 as an attraction for the adjacent **Fanning 66 Outpost and General Store**. It actually rocked for the Guinness Book of World Records, but the rocking motion of a 42-foot tall chair turned out to be so frightening (surprise!) that the owners ended up welding the chair to a base.

Really dwarfed by the world's largest rocking chair

Continuing on from Fanning, we joined Highway

KK in Rosati and took it for almost six miles into the small city of St. James. In St. James (home of the **Vacuum Cleaner Museum**), we returned to Interstate 44—we had a lunch date to make about 12 miles down the road in the city of Rolla and the agreed upon time was coming up quickly!

Friends and Lunch in Rolla

In Rolla (named—really—after Raleigh, North Carolina), we stopped for a very good, extremely filling, and quite relaxed lunch with longtime friends of ours from the Corvette Forum—I've known Greg online for about a decade and we met both Greg and Jolene in person while on a road tour in a *much* older Corvette back in July 2008.

Greg and Jolene were patiently waiting outside as we pulled up to **Joe & Linda's Tater Patch** right off Route 66 on Bridge School Road. After we sat down it shortly became apparent that they knew our waitress from another restaurant—an unexpected plus. The specialty of the house at the more than 40-year-old Tater Patch is (you guessed it!) an absolutely huge potato with a varied set of toppings. Ivelis had the "Broccoli & Cheese Tater" (exactly what it sounds like) while I had the "Tex Mex Tater" (loaded with chili, cheese, onions, and jalapenos). Of course, we both added the butter and sour cream—you might as well just give in …

Greg and Jolene following lunch at the Tater Patch in Rolla

After our very enjoyable lunch with Greg and Jolene, we said our goodbyes, took some pictures, and continued southwest on Martin Springs Drive and Eisenhower Drive through the town of Doolittle (named after and dedicated by General James Harold "Jimmy" Doolittle of World War II Doolittle Raid fame). At that point, we jumped on Interstate 44 for about seven miles where the old route no longer exists. We exited from what Ivelis calls the "superslab" and drove about six miles of the pretty "4-Lane 66" along Highway Z as we headed through the scenic Hooker Cut to the small city of St. Robert.

Scenic "4-Lane 66" near Hooker Cut

Business Loop 44 took us the two miles to the small city of Waynesville (named after United States Army General "Mad" Anthony Wayne from the American Revolutionary War) and past the circa 1903 Pulaski County Courthouse, where we joined Highway 17. A little over a mile further along, we turned right on Highway P and left on Highway L as we traveled about another mile to Laquey (staying on Route 66 in Missouri requires paying close attention and taking a lot of turns).

In Laquey, we took a left on Highway AA, drove about one and a half miles, and took a right onto Highway AB. After six miles, we joined South Outer Road for almost 11 miles through Hazelgreen. We crossed to North Outer Road and headed about five miles to the small city of Lebanon. We stopped for some coffee drinks in Lebanon (home of the circa 1946 **Munger Moss Motel**) before continuing along on first Business Loop 44 for three miles and then on Highway W for almost 10 miles as we headed toward the village of Phillipsburg.

Heading Toward Springfield, Missouri

Near Phillipsburg, we joined Highway C and took

Navigating the Mulhern Way in 2015

Our methods of long-range navigation have changed considerably since the first time we drove Route 66 in 2000. That first time, we had paper maps, Microsoft's Streets & Trips 2000 software running on an IBM ThinkPad 600X, and two now almost classic Nokia cellphones.

By the second trip in 2005, we had moved up to Streets & Trips 2005 with a GPS sensor attached via USB running on an IBM ThinkPad X31, a Palm Treo 650 smartphone (remember those?) with Mapopolis (they're also gone) mapping software—and (still) paper maps.

This time around, things have been almost completely changed by technology that was fairly unimaginable fifteen years ago. Our primary digital navigation method was the TomTom U.S.A. app running on the large screen of Ivelis' iPhone 6 Plus—advantageous because it doesn't need internet connectivity to function (all streets in the United States are stored on-board).

However, wanting to stay on a particular route (such as Route 66) is tough with any modern navigation software—especially if that route is slower or less direct than others.

Luckily there's an *extremely* effective paper alternative; Jerry McClanahan's spiral bound *The EZ66 Guide For Travelers*, currently in its 3rd edition, has turn-by-turn maps and directions, along with mileage counts and other useful features. We relied on it for almost all of our 2,394 miles on Route 66, but will note that *any* effective navigation on Old 66 requires considerable cooperation between navigator and driver.

a quick right onto Highway CC. Highway CC took us almost 19 miles through Conway and Marshfield, where we merged right onto Highway 38 and left onto Highway OO. A little over 12 miles on Highway OO took us to the tiny city of Strafford. We continued straight along Highway OO towards the much larger city of Springfield (our second Springfield along the route). It turns into Kearney Street on the outskirts of town. Shortly after passing the circa 1947 **Rest Haven Court**, we took a left onto Glenstone Avenue, taking the pre-1936 route into the center of Springfield.

The Rest Haven Court on the way into Springfield

Among other things, Springfield is recognized as the "Birthplace of US Route 66," because it was there on April 30, 1926 that officials first proposed that specific designation for the new highway that ran from Chicago to Los Angeles.

Our First Classic Motel Stop on the Trip

In Springfield, we stayed for the night at the **Route 66 Rail Haven** motel a little over two miles south of our turn along Glenstone Avenue. With some portions dating from 1938, the Rail Haven is handsome, well preserved, and (of course) on the National Register of Historic Places.

I credit Best Western for having the sense to help the Rail Haven's franchisees leave well enough alone; there was a palpable and wonderful sense of Route 66 history in many places on the motel grounds. The name Rail Haven is because of the split rail fence that surrounds the property—Elvis Presley and Robert Mitchum both stayed there at various times in the 1950s.

Our room at the Rail Haven was a comfortable size and obviously quite well kept. After I knew we had ourselves reasonably situated at the motel, I took *Louis* out for a much-needed fill-up (we were on our fuel reserve) at a local **Kum & Go** (yes, that's really the name of the 400 plus location chain) about a mile down the road.

Parked quietly in front of our room at the Rail Haven motel in Springfield

Flame Surprises

When I first started planning this trip, our dinner choices in Springfield were an open question. Once we had locked in on staying at the Rail Haven, I did some online exploration and found a steakhouse named **Flame** in the downtown area. The reviews I read were good, so I took a chance and made reservations. We walked almost two miles along first Glenstone Avenue and then East Walnut Street to get to Flame and the walk turned out to be totally worth it.

Our hostess seated us quickly at a stylish booth with leopard-print accents, which made Ivelis quite happy. Both our waiter and bartender were skilled and personable (a good combination!) and the steaks and drinks were excellent—we would definitely visit Flame again.

After a final drink at the restaurant bar, we decided to get a cab back to the Rail Haven; walking another two miles might be a bad idea. You can tell Springfield is a college town (Missouri State University is near the center of the city); when we asked the bartender to call a cab, the immediate response from the dispatcher was "is it cash or credit?" As soon we said "cash," a taxi showed up outside the restaurant *very* quickly.

After just a few minutes in the cab, we were back at the Rail Haven. The two of us settled down pretty quickly for a good night's rest—but not before taking just a few more pictures of the Rail Haven's evocative

Exterior of Flame in Springfield

Neon sign on the grounds of the Rail Haven motel

exterior.

Road Trip Statistics

Miles traveled on our second Route 66 day: **219**
Total travel time: **4 days**
Total miles traveled to this point: **1,318**
Miles from home at the end of this leg (shortest reasonable route): **1,088**

Day 3: from Springfield, MO to Tulsa, OK

Headed Due West

Day three on Route 66 was the actual day of our twentieth wedding anniversary. After a good night's sleep, we woke up refreshed and ready to hit the road. We showered, dressed, packed, and had some strong and hot coffee in the Rail Haven's small and retro office.

It was a nicer day—still cloudy, but not as dreary as the previous day. After I sent a quick tweet (it *is* 2015) to acknowledge our special day, we checked out of the motel in mid-morning, stopped for some supplies at a nearby CVS drug store a little further south on Glenstone Avenue, and headed west towards Kansas and Oklahoma.

As we headed through Springfield proper along East Cherry Street, Ivelis could not resist stopping to take some quick pictures of the Alpha Sigma Alpha sorority house at Missouri State University—she's a sister from her Drexel days. We joined our "correct" Route 66 route on East St Louis Street near the Springfield Expo Center. St Louis Street turns into Park Central East and then Park Central West as you drive around the Park Central Square.

A Quiet Portion of the Route

Park Central West turns into College Street for the next two miles. We drove along College Street, passing what was once the **Rock Fountain Court** on our left as the road fed into the Chestnut Expressway. Once out of Springfield, we headed almost due west for about twenty miles on Missouri Route 266— some quietly pretty driving.

In Paris Springs Junction, we stopped for pictures outside the **Gay Parita Sinclair Station**, created by Gary Turner, who passed in January 2015—I hope his hard work survives.

Replica Sinclair station in Paris Springs Junction

Next was Spencer, where we joined Missouri Route 96 for about thirty miles, passing through Heatonville, Albatross, Phelps, Rescue, Plew, Avilla, and Maxville. From the small town of Maxville, we drove along Old 66 Boulevard for almost two miles before rejoining Missouri Route 96 near the small city of Carthage. As the circa 1939 **Boots Motel** came into view, we took a left on Garrison Street, a right on Oak Street, and passed the old **G&E Tire Company** building with its just a *little* bit dated DeSoto Plymouth sign—DeSoto would come up again for us about 600 miles further down the road.

Old G&E Tire building in Carthage

It was still relatively early in the day, so we drove right on by the **66 Drive-In Theater**, which opened for the first time in 1949 and for the second time in 1998—it's "no trespassing" when they aren't open for business. After driving three miles along Old 66 Boulevard through the village of Brooklyn Heights, we took a few pictures of the handsome brick buildings that house the Webb Corporation, manufacturers of metal fabrication equipment in (natch!) Webb City.

From Webb City we turned left onto South Madison Street, which become North Range Line Road in about a mile as it heads towards the fairly sizable (about 50,000 souls) city of Joplin. A little bit further south along that same road, we had a nice and filling lunch at the busy but comfortable **Granny Shaffer's Family Restaurant**.

Outside Granny Shaffer's in Joplin

After our lunch, we headed south on North Range Line Road for about a mile before taking a right and heading west for five miles along Missouri Route 66 toward the Missouri/Kansas border. Just before the border, we turned right onto Old 66 Boulevard.

Just a Few Miles in Kansas

Kansas is a *tiny* part of Route 66 (only about 13 miles), but we have always found it to be a very worthwhile portion. At the state border Old 66 Boulevard turns into Front Street, which we drove along for a little over a mile into the attractive small city of Galena.

What has changed along the Mother Road in the last few years

Webb Corporation buildings in Webb City

Entering Kansas

Cars On The Route in Galena

Main Street on the outskirts of Galena. **Cars On The Route** is staffed by cool and nice folks—they must get sick of telling stories about *Cars*, but they don't let it show. We'll be sure to stop there again.

Galena was also the first time on this trip, but definitely not the last, that we saw Route 66-specific tour buses—something I do not remember at all from 2000 or 2005.

Don't Miss That Bridge!

In 2005, we somehow missed an essential Route 66 bridge—the **Marsh Rainbow Arch Bridge**—which we *had* managed to find as Route 66 newbies in 2000. Let's just say that we were absolutely *not* going to miss it this time.

We drove south along Main Street in Galena and turned right onto Kansas Highway 66, taking it for four miles into the town of Riverton where we passed the circa 1925 **Williams' Store**. In Riverton, we curved halfway through a traffic circle onto Beasley Road. We continued down Beasley Road for

that we saw first in Kansas is the marked influence of Disney's wonderful and obsessively detailed *Cars* movie, which was released in June 2006 and was heavily based on Route 66 locations. Our first sign of this was a version of Tow Mater named Tow Tater (Disney definitely does protect their trademarks!) in Galena parked at a nicely restored Kan-O-Tex gas station (circa 1934) at the corner of Front Street and

Ivelis, *Louis*, two nice Kansas kids, and the Marsh Rainbow Arch bridge in Riverton

about a mile until we could see the bridge off in the distance—only at this point did I have any confidence that we wouldn't miss it again!

As we pulled up to the bridge (otherwise known as the Bush Creek Bridge) to take some beauty shots, a pickup truck pulled up on the other side. A *much* younger couple, likely of high school age, got out. They were quite polite, as we have found most Kansans. I told them that we would be out of their way shortly; the young man told me that it definitely wasn't a problem and asked if we were members of any of the local Corvette clubs. I told that we weren't because we were from the Philadelphia area—they both seemed impressed.

After getting our pictures on the bridge, we said goodbye to the young couple and headed due south along 50th Street for almost three miles toward the center of the small city of Baxter Springs. 50th Street becomes Willow Street—we curved left onto 3rd Street and turned right onto Military Avenue.

Baxter Springs

In Baxter Springs, we stopped for a few minutes at a beautifully restored brick and stucco cottage-style **Phillips 66 Station** on the corner of 10th Street, which is on the National Register of Historic Places and serves as the local visitor's center. While we were inside the circa 1930 building, one of the gentleman working there gave us some *very* specific information on where it might be a *really* good idea to slow down a little over the next several miles—I guess seeing and hearing *Louis* made him think we might be able to use the advice!

Restored Phillips 66 station in Baxter Springs

One of the interesting things that happens as one heads into the mid-west is that the folks working at the *real* McDonald's fast food restaurants you stop at begin to be as nice as they are in the national commercials. We made it a point to stop yet again at the wonderful Baxter Springs McDonald's a little further down on Military Avenue—we actually entered from the Old 66 Route on Roberts Road. After enjoying an afternoon snack, we drove a little less than one mile due south into Oklahoma.

We crossed into Oklahoma in the mid-afternoon just north of the town of Quapaw. We followed first US 69A and than US 69 for about ten miles into the tiny city of Commerce. Commerce was Hall of Fame baseball player Mickey Mantle's hometown, so, appropriately, we followed Mickey Mantle Boulevard into the center of town. We took a right onto Commerce Street and a left onto Main Street. After almost a mile, we rejoined US 69 in North Miami, driving a little over three miles into Miami proper, home of both the famous circa 1929 Spanish Revival **Coleman Theater** and **Waylan's Ku-Ku Burger**.

The only remaining Ku-Ku Burger, in Miami

Traveling the Ribbon Road

Next, we drove the somewhat scary (especially in a low-slung sports car like ours) but *very* historic "Ribbon Road" (also known as the "Sidewalk Highway") that exists for about six miles between Miami and Afton. The "Ribbon Road" is a nine-foot wide length of highway with a concrete base and curbs and an asphalt surface that served as the Route 66 route from 1922 to 1937. Not surprisingly, it is disintegrating after all those years—we drove quite slowly, especially at the 90-degree corners! Upon exiting at the south end, we were rewarded with a commemorative marker for our troubles.

Passenger's view of "Ribbon Road" between Miami and Afton

After finishing our time on the ribbon road we entered Afton, passing the ruins of the **Rest Haven Motel** and the **Afton Motel**. We followed US 69 and US 60 for about 15 miles to the small city of Vinita.

After Vinita, we headed a few miles west on Oklahoma Highway 66 through White Oak before continuing southwest on the same route for 30 miles through Chelsea (passing the remains of the **Chelsea Motel**), Bushyhead, Foyil (home of **Ed Galloway's Totem Pole Park**), and Sequoyah towards the city of Claremore (named after Will Rogers' father Clem Rogers).

The Rest Haven sign in ruin, Afton

The Blue Whale of Catoosa

From Claremore, it's about 13 miles to Catoosa on Oklahoma 66. We took a quick right from 66—you really have to be ready for it or you'll be making a u-turn somewhere down the road—to visit the *fabulous* **Blue Whale of Catoosa**, created (very appropriately in our view on this particular day) as an anniversary gift. As the personable attendant at the gift shop nearby stated, he is looking great—the positive changes since we first visited in 2000 cannot be overstated. In addition to the now very well maintained whale, there is a seating area, and the ark next door (fenced off and falling apart for many years) is now being worked on.

Ivelis visits with the fabulous Blue Whale of Catoosa

After our absolutely essential visit with the blue whale, we got back on Oklahoma 66. We missed one of the many turns in Catoosa and decided to "punt", launching the TomTom app on Ivelis' iPhone and asking it to provide the quickest possible route to our hotel in Tulsa. It responded by getting us on Interstate 44 for four miles and then on Interstate 244 for six miles, getting us off on Harvard Avenue for a little less than a mile, and taking a right back onto Route 66 with less than a mile to our destination.

Finally Getting the Accommodations Right

For our actual twentieth wedding anniversary night, we stayed at **The Campbell Hotel**, a restored and very cool boutique hotel dating from 1927 that is right on Route 66 in downtown Tulsa.

It was quite hot when we arrived in Tulsa—sunny and in the upper eighties. We parked *Louis* behind the hotel, unloaded, and enjoyed the air conditioning in our room, provided by the same Mitsubishi units that we had in our own house for many years.

Our beautifully furnished and decorated room in the Campbell was number 203—the Bama Suite—named after the Bama Pie Company, a Tulsa legend that dates from the Great Depression and is still in operation. These snazzy accommodations were a major victory for me on this Route 66 trip—on our two previous trips, I had timed our nightly stops badly, placing us in fairly basic motels on our anniversary night. This seems to bother me much more than it bothers Ivelis, but I wanted to get it right this time—and I definitely believe I did.

Lobby of The Campbell Hotel in Tulsa

We had dinner that evening at a Fleming's Steakhouse in the Utica Square shopping center, which turned out to be another two-mile walk—for a trip that was supposed to be all about driving, we were doing a *lot* of walking! I'll freely acknowledge that choosing any national steak chain was somewhat of a "punt" on any Route 66 trip, but we *really* like Fleming's (there's one about five miles from where we live) and I wasn't willing to take any risks with the dining on our anniversary after *finally* getting the lodging right.

As I expected, Fleming's did not disappoint—we had a very nice and relaxed dinner before walking outside into the fading light and calling an UberX (it *is* 2015). A very nice lady named Anne came quickly in her GMC Terrain (I notice these things) and drove us back to our hotel, where we had one last drink at the stylish bar and went happily upstairs to sleep.

Road Trip Statistics

Miles travelled on our third Route 66 day: **197**
Total travel time: **5 days**
Total miles traveled to this point: **1,519**
Miles from home at the end of this leg (shortest reasonable route): **1,266**

Route 66, Day 4: from Tulsa, OK to Tucumcari, NM

The morning to mid-afternoon drive from Tulsa to Erick

A Full Day Traveling the Mother Road

Early the next morning, Ivelis and I woke up in our comfortable and rather luxurious suite at The Campbell Hotel. After showering and dressing, we had a good breakfast at the restaurant adjacent to the hotel, finished our packing, and checked out shortly thereafter.

The way the timing had worked out on this trip meant that this particular day was going to be one of the longest of our eight days on Route 66. We needed to travel almost 500 miles to from Tulsa to Tucumcari, New Mexico and I also had *many* stops planned on the way; Oklahoma's central and southwest regions have much to offer the modern traveler of Route 66.

Our hotel was located right on Old 66, so we simply exited the parking lot, made a left turn, and headed west toward the center of Tulsa along 11th Street for a little less than two miles, passing the distinctive **Meadow Gold** sign (recently saved and relocated by a host of Tulsa entities) along the way. We curved left and went two-thirds of the way through a roundabout before joining 10th Street. Five blocks further along, we rejoined 11th Street and quickly curved onto 12th Street.

Leaving Tulsa

We took a left onto Southwest Boulevard and crossed the Arkansas River—the once gorgeous **11th Street Arkansas River Bridge** is not currently passable; a recent analysis deemed it "... too expensive to repair, too historic to demolish, and too valuable to ignore."

About two miles south of the bridge, we passed the magnificent **Meteor 4500** steam engine, which is one of three Baldwin locomotives that ran the *Meteor* route (with its "Air-Conditioned Sleeping Cars") from St. Louis to Oklahoma City in the 1940s—the period immediately before the momentous and rather painful transition to diesel engines.

We continued along Southwest Boulevard for about

Recently moved MeadowGold sign on the way into Tulsa

The Meteor 4500 steam engine in Tulsa

nine miles through Red Fork, Oakhurst, and Bowden. Near the city of Sapulpa and it's **Bridge #18 at Rock Creek**, we took a right onto Oklahoma 66, which we followed for the next 23 miles or so, passing through Kellyville, Bellvue, and heading into the tiny city of Bristow.

From Bristow, we continued on Oklahoma 66 for about 17 miles through Depew, Stroud (with the classic **Skyliner Motel** sign present right in the middle of town), Davenport, and Chandler. From Chandler (allegedly the "Pecan Capital of the World"), we continued through Warwick and crossed under Interstate 44 on our way towards the town of Wellston.

Skyliner Motel sign in Stroud

The Only Round Barn …

We took Highway 66B through Wellston, rejoining Oklahoma 66 on our way past the town of Luther to the tiny town of Arcadia. Arcadia's famous round barn (built in 1898 and somehow the only round barn on Route 66) is the absolute definition of a Route 66 photo opportunity. We stopped to take photos that turned out to be *very* close in composition to the ones we had taken back in 2005.

Parked outside the round barn in Arcadia

Traveling Together After Twenty Years

Ivelis and I have taken a *lot* of multi-day road trips together in the last 20 years. Over that time, we've developed a few traveling tips that help us move along with a minimum of fuss.

Our first tip seems obvious: it is to only pack clothes that we expect to wear. In practice, this means that Ivelis packs a few comfortable, low-maintenance dresses (she currently favors the ones from TravelSmith) and I pack khaki trousers, shirts that go well with them, and a blazer for when the two of us need to be a little bit more dressy.

Our second tip is to take care of as much as possible in the evening instead of the next morning. Filling up the fuel tank and getting any needed supplies is often much easier in the early evening than in the early morning—and we are also more likely to remember what we actually need.

Our third and final tip is to set reasonable driving times for each day on the road. Though she's willing to get up *quite* early, Ivelis strongly prefers to be wherever we are going to stop for the night well before dark and, over time, I have come to agree with her.

After our stop at the barn, Ivelis and I decided that we definitely needed to "make some time," so I found a way to navigate us around Oklahoma City by taking Interstate 35 south and joining Interstate 40 heading west.

We rejoined old 66 in El Reno, driving along Sunset Drive toward Fort Reno. After Fort Reno, we drove along "2-Lane 66" for a little over 11 miles before joining first the US 281 Spur for a little over two miles and then picking up US 281 itself as we headed past Hinton Junction about two miles towards the small town of Bridgeport.

Once we were past Bridgeport (population 116), we followed Oklahoma 66 for approximately 11 miles to Hydro (a reference to that town's plentiful well water), where we got back on the North Frontage Road and headed about five miles toward Weatherford.

Two Excellent Museums in Southwestern Oklahoma

We've driven right on by it two times prior: on this trip we were *definitely* going to visit the **Stafford Air & Space Museum** in the small city of Weatherford. Named after Weatherford native Lieutenant General Thomas P. Stafford (who had an amazing aerospace career that included Gemini 6A, Gemini 9A, Apollo 10, and the Apollo-Soyuz Test Project), this museum is completely unexpected in its small-town location but *really* impressive.

Huge Rocketdyne F-1 in the Stafford Air & Space Museum

Just a few highlights of the museum's over 3,000 artifacts include a Bell X-1 rocket plane and a General Dynamics F-16 fighter—General Stafford oversaw the research and development program for the F-16. There's also a replica Gemini spacecraft capsule, a Titan II rocket, a Rocketdyne F-1 from the third stage of a Saturn V rocket, and the hatch through which U.S. astronauts and Russian cosmonauts docked and greeted each other in space during the Apollo-Soyuz mission. Ivelis and I lingered for a good bit longer at the museum than I had planned, but I had no regrets.

Replica Gemini spacecraft capsule—so small!

After leaving the Stafford Air & Space Museum, we followed Main Street as it turned into East Davis Avenue. A mile down the road, we turned left onto Washington Avenue. About a mile further, we returned to Interstate 40 for about ten miles before rejoining the Mother Road as we exited onto Gary Boulevard west of Clinton. We followed Gary Boulevard for almost four miles as we drove though almost all of the small city of Clinton.

Before leaving Clinton, we stopped once again at the wonderful **Oklahoma Route 66 Museum** on Gary Boulevard. The museum is the same, but yet different, from the way it was ten years ago, with the well-designed exhibits continuously being updated and upgraded. Both of us continue to stand by our opinion that it is the best of the *many* Route 66 museums that exist—it actually isn't even the only one in Oklahoma. Perhaps there are too many Route 66 museums …

Ivelis and I took a little over an hour to view the various exhibits, which are set in chronological order. After that, we spent some time and money at the museum's small but interesting gift shop—Ivelis prevailed upon me to buy a Hawaiian-style Route

66-themed shirt, she got a set of cheap sunglasses, and we purchased some souvenir shirts for a few of the young children in our lives. Afterwards, we left the museum and headed south along Gary Boulevard for about a half a mile.

Outside the wondrous Oklahoma Route 66 Museum

Now at least somewhat conscious of the passage of time and the need to get to Tucumcari before dark, we got back on Interstate 40 and headed for the Oklahoma/Texas border, traveling about 65 miles through Foss, Canute, Elk City, Sayre, Hext, Erick, and Texola.

Entering Texas just west of Texaola

Here Comes the Panhandle

Just past the *absolutely tiny* town of Texola (population 47), we crossed into the Texas panhandle. About 14 miles past the border in the tiny city of Shamrock, we stopped at a McDonald's for a quick and quite late lunch and (of course) some more coffee—I absolutely *inhale* coffee on our longer driving days. We also filled *Louis* up at a Chevron conveniently located right down the street.

After getting back on the road, we passed through Lela, McLean (both the last town in Texas bypassed by Interstate 40 and the home of the **Texas Route 66 Museum**), and Alanreed. Shortly after Alanreed (named after Messrs. Alan and Reed), all travelers must join Interstate 40 for about eight miles—there's nothing else left.

Deliberately leaning water tower in Groom

Next came Jericho, followed by the small town of Groom. Groom will be forever noted for a water tower that was deliberately placed with a definite lean—the goal being to get travelers to leave the highway, visit the Britten restaurant and truck stop, ask about that leaning water tower, and (hopefully) buy something. After passing Groom, we headed through Conway on our way towards Amarillo,

The mid-afternoon to evening drive from Erick to Tucumcari

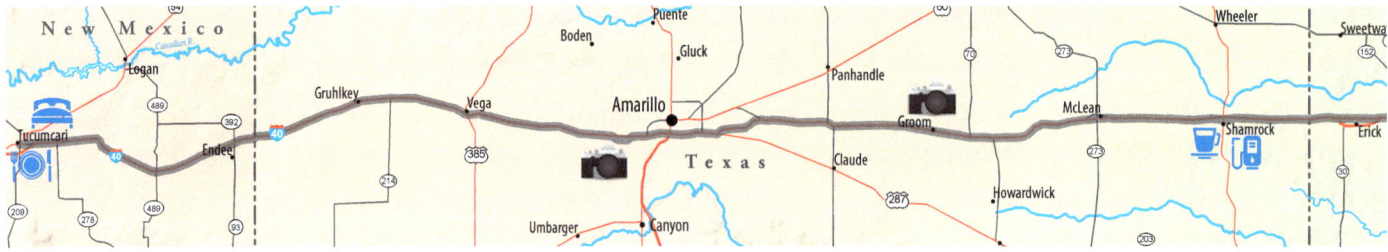

Louis pauses just outside the Cadillac Ranch in Amarillo

which at about 190,000 is by far the largest city in the Texas panhandle.

It was quite windy on our route in Texas: in fact, wind ended up being the defining weather characteristic of this entire trip. Our particular Route 66 "rules" said that we absolutely *had* to stop for some pictures outside the **Cadillac Ranch** in the western outskirts of Amarillo—so we did. As I took the photos, I thought back to the Cadillac-based flower sculptures that we had seen in downtown Chicago over a thousand miles prior.

Tucumcari Tonite!

Following our stop at the Cadillac Ranch, Ivelis and I headed toward the Texas/New Mexico border, passing through Bushland, Wildorado, Vega (home of the circa 1947 **Vega Motel** and not much else), and the tiny city of Adrian. Past Adrian (which competes with Vega for the distinction of being at the exact midpoint of Route 66), there is once again no choice but to get on Interstate 40 and stay on it all the way to the border—as we neared it, we began to see the famous and at this point quite reassuring "Tucumcari tonite!" signs.

The Tucumcari Tonite! signs are back

Ivelis and I crossed into New Mexico near the ghost town of Glenrio and proceeded fairly swiftly along Interstate 40 for almost 40 miles through Endee, Bard, and San Jon on our way to the small city of Tucumcari. We exited onto Tucumcari Boulevard and headed two miles into the center of Tucumcari, driving past the interesting **Historic Route 66 Motel** (built in the 1960s in the International Style) and the circa 1953 **Palomino Motel** on the way to our particular stop for the night.

There was more change in Tucumcari: of the 1950s era **Pony Soldier Motel** only the sign remains—the actual motel was finally demolished in 2010. With an assist from its excellent location, Tucumcari hangs on far better than most, but at least some continued loss seems inevitable.

Only the Pony Soldier sign remains

We Finally Actually Stay at the Blue Swallow

After many years of thinking, talking, and (yes!) dreaming about it, Ivelis and I finally actually *stayed* at the famous and gorgeous **Blue Swallow Motel** along on old 66 in Tucumcari. Currently *extremely* well run by Nancy and Kevin Mueller, the Blue Swallow is absolutely amazing and, of course, is on the National Register of Historic Places. It opened for business in 1941 and has been a Route 66 treasure ever since.

After we had pulled up in front of the motel office, Kevin made a point of showing me our room (#2)—as if we were going to object! After seeing that I was absolutely fine with our beautifully maintained accommodations for the night, he asked if we had any dinner plans. I mentioned that we intended to visit the **Pow Wow Restaurant & Lizard Lounge** and Kevin gave me an appropriate coupon and mentioned that they offered a Blue Swallow margarita (of course!).

After *very* carefully parking in the admittedly tiny garage next to our room and getting quickly settled, we walked about a mile west along Route 66 to the Pow Wow for dinner, passing several other motels of note, including the circa 1959 **Motel Safari**.

Motel Safari in Tucumcari

Eating and Drinking at the Pow Wow

Those who know Ivelis well will not be very surprised to know that she actually ordered the previously discussed Blue Swallow margarita as soon as we arrived at Pow Wow. This particular concoction turned out to be *really* good, so she ended up ordering a couple more of them over the course of the evening. The food at the Pow Wow Restaurant was also quite good—Ivelis enjoyed her beef fajitas and I enjoyed every bit of my food and drink.

After finishing our meal, we spent a little while longer having a few more drinks at the Lizard Lounge bar with a woman both of us think is likely the proprietor.

Blue Swallow margarita

Night Falls in Tucumcari

With Tucumcari's magnificently preserved bright neon painting light all around us (even the local **Boulevard Cleaners and Laundromat** has really nice neon!), we walked back east along Route 66 to the Blue Swallow. We began to settle in for the night, but not before getting some fairly wonderful pictures (they turned out *much* better than I thought they would).

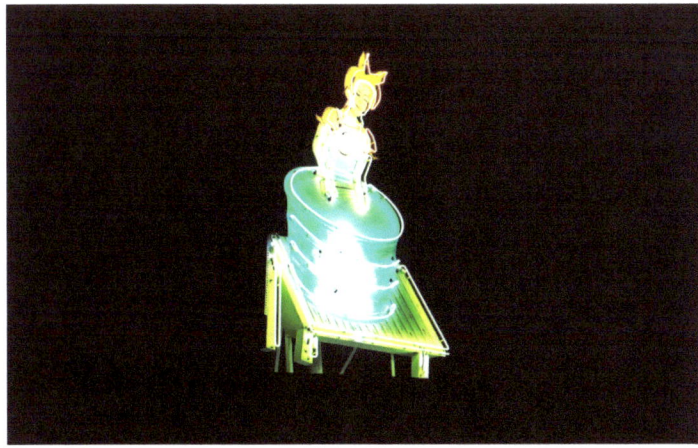

In Tucumcari even the local laundromat has gorgeous neon

Our exceptionally preserved room had many amazing touches, including an ancient but working rotary telephone (made functional with a grant from CenturyLink).

Glorious neon—the Blue Swallow in Tucumcari all lit up

It had been a long day and it was starting to get late. Ivelis announced that she was going to go to sleep. I told her that was absolutely fine, but honesty

Automotive News from 1958

required me to admit to her that I was going to read the entire length of the *Automotive News* from the week of September 22nd, 1958 that had been placed on my nightstand. Ivelis giggled and turned off her light.

I actually *did* read the entire paper from front to back before turning off my light and going to sleep. After the two of us had passed the DeSoto sign in Carthage on the previous day, one of the articles in this particular *Automotive News* detailed how hopeful DeSoto dealers were for the new 1959 model year—DeSoto would barely make into the 1960s, folding suddenly in late 1961. In 1959, the most expensive car available for sale in the United States was a Ferrari 250 GT—at about $14,000 (a nice 1959 250 GT is worth approximately *$750,000* in late 2015).

Road Trip Statistics

Miles traveled on our fourth Route 66 day: **483**
Total travel time: **6 days**
Total miles traveled to this point: **2,002**
Miles from home at the end of this leg (shortest reasonable route): **1,739**

Day 5: from Tucumcari, NM to Sante Fe, NM

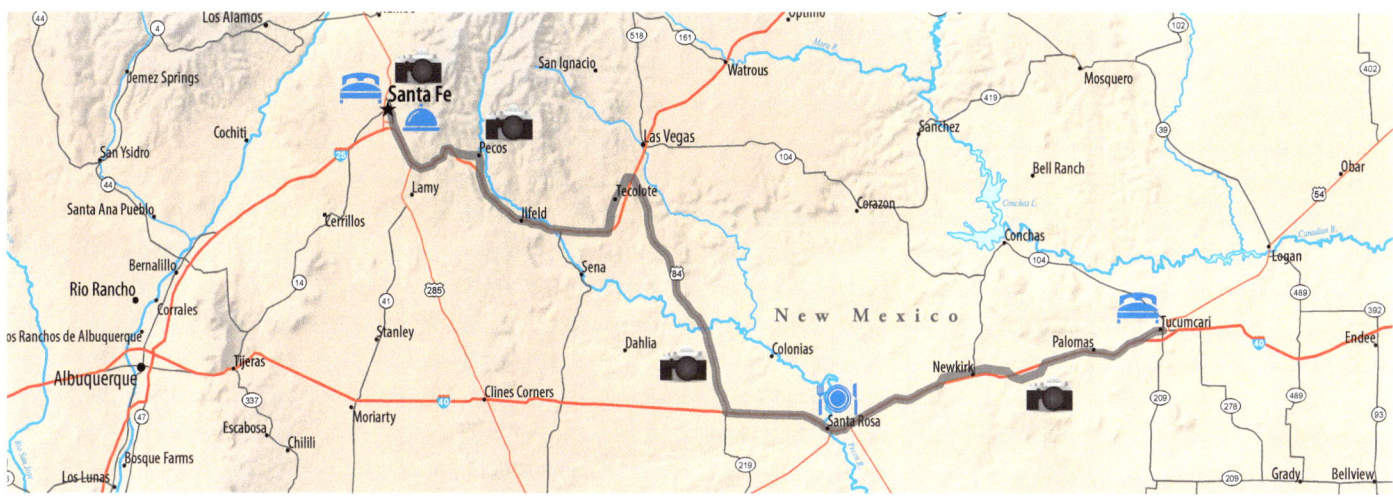

Beginning a Shorter Driving Day

The next morning, we woke up early, dressed, and packed. Ivelis and I drank some hot and strong coffee in the Blue Swallow's office, took a few more pictures, and bought some souvenirs. One of the souvenirs we purchased was a motel key tag with our room number on it (of course we also got one with 66 on it). Our host Kevin told us a great story about how he was sorting through a profusion of key tags one day and people kept trying to buy them—suddenly an opportunity for commerce became a little more obvious …

After visiting a little while longer with Nancy and Kevin, we got back in *Louis* and reluctantly left the Blue Swallow. The first part of this day's relatively short drive involved getting on Interstate 40 as we exited from the west portion of Tucumcari—Route 66 is often almost completely gone in some parts of eastern New Mexico. About 18 miles down the road, we exited onto the South Frontage Road in Montoya, site of the long-closed and now disintegrating **Richardson Store** (built in the mid to late 1920s) and a few other remnants.

The old road curves several miles west of Tucumcari

We drove along for six more miles before crossing over the interstate onto the North Frontage Road for another 14 miles through Newkirk and to the ghost town of Cuervo. In Cuervo, we rejoined Interstate 40 for 14 miles as we headed towards the small city of Santa Rosa (where the train scene in film version of *The Grapes Of Wrath* was shot).

Souvenirs from the Blue Swallow

Stopping in Santa Rosa

It had been a couple of hours on the road. We exited the interstate onto Will Rogers Drive on the eastern outskirts of Santa Rosa (known as the "City of Natural Lakes" because of the various artesian springs in the area) and drove a little over two miles before filling up *Louis* at a Shell. Just across the street was the 25-acre **Park Lake Historic District**—an artifact of the 1930s Works Progress Administration (WPA).

About a half a mile further west of the Shell, we stopped for a leisurely and filling breakfast at **Joseph's Bar & Grill**—open since 1956 and the current home of the long gone **Club Café**'s famous Fat Man logo.

After finishing our breakfast, we drove about a mile back east to visit the **Route 66 Auto Museum**, an interesting and *very* eclectic collection of cars, including some for sale, owned by local entrepreneur James "Bozo" Cordova and his wife Anna.

We turned back west along Will Rogers Drive, which becomes Route 66 about two miles further along as it crosses the Pecos River. About a mile later, we rejoined Interstate 40 for 17 miles—Old 66 in this area is now largely found on private lands.

Some Lonely and Beautiful Miles

Next, we turned north-northwest along lonely Route 84 at exit 256 as we followed the *far* less direct pre-1937 route otherwise known as the "Santa Fe Loop." We drove about 42 miles under bright blue skies along Route 84 though Dilia before exiting onto the Frontage Road near Romeroville.

Ivelis and I proceeded a little over 19 miles through Tecolote, Bernal, and San Jose before crossing under Interstate 25 and getting on the South Frontage Road. Another 12 miles or so further along and we had passed Sands and Ilfield. In the village of Rowe, we turned north and headed along Highway 63 for a little over five miles as we followed a mid-1970s Ford pickup truck into Pecos.

In what passes for the downtown of Pecos (a village of 1,441), we took a hard left onto Highway 50 and drove about six miles to Glorieta (population 859), where we encountered some significant construction

Heading towards Santa Fe along Route 84

Following an old Ford pickup truck into Pecos

on our planned route. At this point, we joined Interstate 25 and headed about 19 miles straight into old Santa Fe.

Continuing along the pre-1937 route

Happily Back in Santa Fe

Ivelis and I arrived in Santa Fe late in the morning, so we had plenty of time to enjoy the historic downtown on a slightly chilly but quite beautiful day—Santa Fe (long known as the "City Different") is on my rather short list of cities that I would happily move to if the right opportunity came along.

After several twists and turns along some old streets, we parked *Louis* in our hotel's lot, verified that our room was not yet ready (perfectly reasonable at that time of day but still worth the check), and walked a few blocks into the absolute center of town, which includes the *very* historic **Santa Fe Plaza** (circa 1610 and on the National Register of Historic Places).

One of the many reasons that Ivelis was so eager to visit Santa Fe again is the wonderful **Back at the Ranch** cowboy boot store on East Marcy Street, so we headed a few blocks over in that direction. Ivelis carefully evaluated her *many* options while I talked with the store's owner, discovering that she hails from a town only about ten miles from our house (small world). After just a little hemming and hawing, Ivelis decided on some ostrich three-quarter length black boots—I think they're gorgeous.

Ivelis' new boots

After just a little more perambulating around the old downtown, we had a light lunch and some really good drinks at the **Thunderbird Bar & Grill**, which directly overlooks the Santa Fe Plaza. Afterwards, we relaxed for a couple of hours in our "King Deluxe Poolview" room (I'm *eternally* amused by hotel room categories) at the really nice **Hilton Santa Fe Historic Plaza**, which opened in 1973 and is partially housed

Outside our hotel in Santa Fe

in a hacienda originally built in 1625.

Geronimo Astounds, Again

In the early evening, we requested an Uber vehicle and headed a little over a mile east (maybe we'll walk it next time) to dinner at **Geronimo**, a restaurant on Canyon Road which we've been talking about (really!) since we last ate there ten years ago in April 2005. Located in the Borrego House, which dates from 1756 (Sante Fe is *not* a young city by American standards), Geronimo was once again absolutely superlative in food, drinks, ambiance, and service—perhaps the best restaurant that we've been to west of the Mississippi River in the United States.

Excellent food lives here

When we're at Geronimo, we try to leave our food comfort zones at least a little bit—Ivelis chose the elk tenderloin as her main course and vastly enjoyed it. For dessert, I took a very successful flyer on their trio of crème brûlée; espresso, raspberry, and vanilla.

My trio of crème brûlée at Geronimo

When dinner was over, we requested Uber again and got the same SUV (Toyota Sequoia) and driver (Fabian) that had brought us *to* Geronimo. I don't think there a lot of Uber drivers working in Santa Fe—at least not in early April.

After getting back to our hotel, we walked across the street to the relatively new AGAVE Lounge in the **Eldorado Hotel** (where we've stayed before) for a nightcap. Afterwards, we headed back to the Hilton and slept very comfortably in our stylish, comfortable, and expansive room.

Road Trip Statistics

Miles traveled on our fifth Route 66 day: **185**
Total travel time: **7 days**
Total miles traveled to this point: **2,187**
Miles from home at the end of this leg (shortest reasonable route): **1,906**

Day 6: from Sante Fe, NM to Holbrook, AZ

The morning drive from Santa Fe to Continental Divide

Reluctantly Leaving Santa Fe

After our wonderful afternoon and evening in Santa Fe—about 350 miles, we woke up the next morning with some driving to do. We showered, packed, checked out of the hotel, and headed out to the car. As Ivelis and I were loading our luggage into *Louis*, I managed to somehow *completely* miss a chance at photographing an old four engine propeller aircraft that passed almost directly overhead us. Sigh …

We followed Cerrellos Road out of Santa Fe (passing the circa 1936 **El Rey Court**—now the **El Rey Inn**) for several miles until it joined Interstate 25 heading southwest. We stayed on the interstate for about twenty miles until we reached Algodones where we joined Old 66 on Highway 313 and headed several miles further to the town of Bernallilo and breakfast.

A Truly Great Breakfast

In downtown Bernallilo, we stopped at the **Range Café** right on Route 66 right after Calle Don Francisco. After nearly parking in tow zones not once but twice, we finally parked in the *correct* location across the street and entered this very well recommended restaurant with high hopes. The Range Café's slogan is "Ordinary Food Done Extraordinarily Well!" and they certainly delivered on this promise—I believe this was the best breakfast of the trip (and we had many good breakfasts).

Our personable waitress was named Celeste and she

Vintage El Rey Court postcard

Walking toward the excellent Range Café

Inside the Range Café

took really good care of us. Just to give the reader an idea (and perhaps make some a little hungry), Ivelis had the "Kitchen Sink" (a three egg omelet with ham, bacon, white cheddar, cream cheese, green onion, avocado, and tomato with fruit, fries, and toast on the side) and I had the blue corn pancakes with blueberries and toasted piñon (an edible pine seed) with bacon on the side. A little over an hour later, we left the restaurant absolutely stuffed and *very* happy—we would eagerly visit any of the Range Café's three locations again.

Inexact Memory When Retaking a Long Route

It's very interesting to me what one's memory does when you take the same long route multiple times over a few decades.

The first way my memory is inexact is around distance. For some reason, I had some very precise memories of Route 66 distances that turned out to be completely wrong when we actually took the trip.

My second form of inexact memory is order. Especially as we went further west along the Mother Road, I found myself becoming confused about which sights came before each other.

Finally, both Ivelis and I repeated pictures from the same angle that we had taken them in previous trips—even when just taking quick snapshots of interesting signs. There are several pictures we took on this trip that are nearly exact duplicates of pictures we took in 2000 or 2005.

Staying on the Pre-1937 Route

On this trip, we had the hours and days available to take significantly more of the older route than we ever had before. So, instead of taking the traditional right turn (as per Bugs Bunny) at Albuquerque, we continued to follow the pre-1937 route and headed south through the center of that fairly large city—at 557,000, Albuquerque is now the 32nd largest city in the United States.

KiMo Theater sign

After passing the **El Camino Motor Hotel** and the circa 1927 "Pueblo Deco" **KiMo Theater** in the city center, we continued south along Isleta Boulevard for about eight miles through Armijo, Parajito, and Los Padillos. We crossed Interstate 25 and traveled about two more miles on Isleta Boulevard.

In Isleta Pueblo (where Thomas Edison made the first motion picture in 1898), we joined Highway 47 for seven miles through Bosque Farms, Peralta, and Valencia stopping at a drug store for some sundries before entering the large village of Los Lunas (named after the Luna family who originally settled the area).

In Los Lunas (home of famous blues guitarist Bo Diddley for most of the 1970s), we turned northwest along Highway 6, where we followed a modified white C6 Corvette and a white sixties Cadillac sedan for a little while.

After we exited Los Lunas, things thinned out rapidly—we drove 34 miles and joined Interstate 40 near the ghost town of Correo (Correo is a Spanish word meaning "mail"—Googling it brings up Gmail as the first hit). Ivelis and I traveled along the superhighway through Mesita, Budville (home of an old trading post with a sordid history), and the ghost

Following a Corvette and a Cadillac through Los Lunas

for almost 34 miles through Milan, Bluewater, Prewitt, and Thoreau (*not* named for Henry David Thoreau). Just like both of our previous trips, we stopped at **Continental Divide** to take the obligatory photos and got back on Interstate 40—there's no other option.

Pausing at Continental Divide

town of McCarty's.

We exited onto Highway 117 and heading about five miles into the city of Grants, which was named after three Canadian brothers whose last name was Grant—thus the plural. In downtown Grants, we viewed many classic signs, including those of the **Sands Motel**, **Grants Cafe**, **West Theatre**, and **Los Alamitos Motel**.

Next, we traveled on Highway 122

Grants—only the sign remains

Arizona Beckons

About twenty miles down the road, we exited just east of the city of Gallup. In Gallup, we filled up with premium at a Shell gas station before stopping for some coffee drinks. We also viewed Gallup's many cool old motels and other attractions as we drove slowly through the town, with the road parallel to the old Santa Fe Railroad train tracks.

Of note near the Gallup city center is the large and impressive **El Rancho Hotel & Motel** which was built in 1936, has *gloriously* uninhibited interior decor, and was often a stopping place for movie stars such as Clark Gable and John Wayne—I'd love to

The afternoon drive from Continental Divide to Holbrook

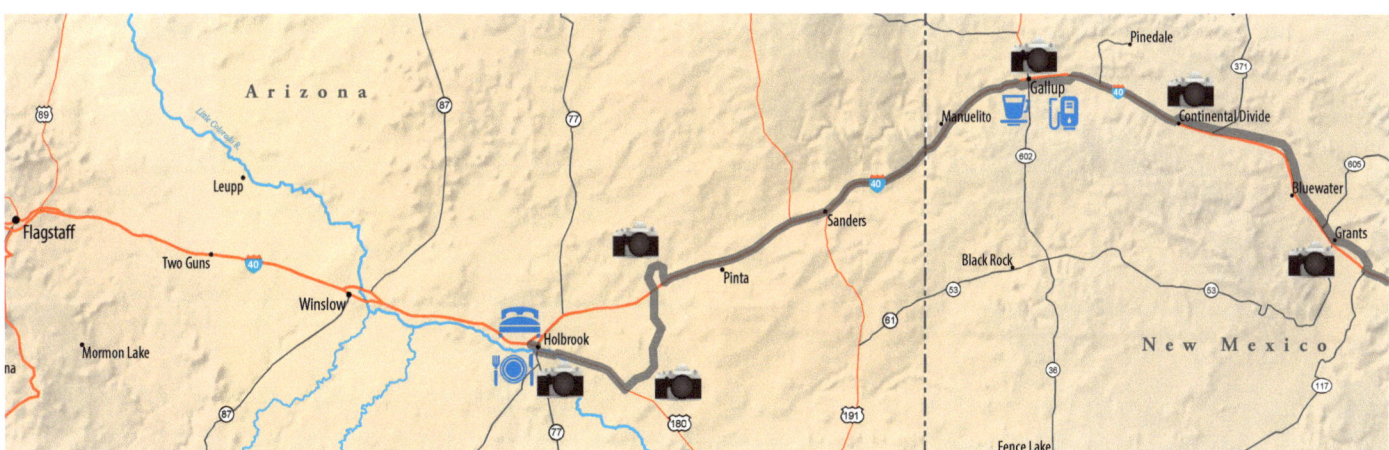

stay there some day. From Gallup, we headed southwest for about 17 lonely miles to the New Mexico/Arizona border.

We crossed the border into Arizona near Lupton (population all of 25) in the early afternoon. Old 66 is largely obliterated and/or on private lands in the extreme eastern part of the state, so we "made time" for about 50 miles along Interstate 40. We passed through Allentown, Houck, Querino, Chambers, and Navajo as we headed rapidly toward our next and highly anticipated stop.

El Rancho sign in Gallup

The Natural Awesomeness of the Petrified Forest

After exiting at Park Road and stopping for a few minutes at the visitors center to secure a park map, we paid David the park ranger our $10 and entered the **Petrified Forest National Park** at exactly 3:45 PM. The first two times we visited this amazing park were in the morning and we were really interested in how seeing it in the afternoon would be different. We powered down our side windows and started our slow drive through the park.

President Theodore Roosevelt designated the park as national monument way back in 1906. If you are travelling from the east, this large (about 350 square miles) and stunningly gorgeous park begins in the Painted Desert portion. We drove along for a few miles before stopping at a quiet and small overlook between Tiponi Point and Tawa Point to take some pictures …

After those first beauty shots in the park (another of which accompanies the author's note at the beginning of this book), we drove along, passing the **Painted Desert Inn** which was built by the

Looking out over the painted desert

Painted Desert Inn

big finish—the huge fallen trees in the Giant Logs portion of the Petrified Forest. After stopping for several minutes, we exited the park and headed northwest along US 180 towards Holbrook for about ten miles.

Civilian Conservation Corps in the late 1930s. A few miles futher down the park road, we stopped at the haunting crossover of old Route 66 that's pictured on this book's title page—telephone poles heading off towards nothing.

While we were stopped at the crossover, we met young Manuel and Jenny (was *every* couple we were meeting for the first time on this trip notably younger than us?) and their *very* impressive black Lingenfelter Camaro as they headed east.

A huge tree in the Petrified Forest National Park

A Night at the Wigwam

After waiting a little while for a long freight train to pass at another train crossing, we arrived at another iconic Route 66 motel, the **Wigwam** in Holbrook, in the late afternoon. Built in 1950 and one of seven related motels, the Wigwam is a collection of fifteen concrete tepees, each of them fourteen feet in diameter and each of them serving as an individual motel room. There are various old cars parked throughout the location; a rather immense (over 18 foot long—slightly longer than today's Bentley Mulsanne *sedan*) white 1972 Lincoln Continental Mark IV coupe was parked just outside our room.

Once I had checked us in and we had gotten rea-

Our Centennial meets a Lingenfelter Camaro

Manuel made me smile because he instantly recognized our rather specific Corvette version—"Is that a Centennial Edition?", he said. I allowed as to that it was and that there certainly wasn't anything wrong with their Camaro or the motor that was sitting under its hood. After taking pictures of each other's cars and talking for a few more minutes, we headed off in opposite directions.

Next, we crossed under Interstate 40 and headed first south and then southwest towards the park's

Louis nestled between a Chevrolet and a huge Lincoln

sonably settled in our room, we walked about half a mile east from the Wigwam to what turned out to be a small, simple, but *really* good Mexican restaurant named **Romo's**—this was evidently one of our days for great food. As we looked over the food menu, I took a quick gander at the beer card at the center of our small two-top. All the expected mass-market beers were listed (Coors Light, Budweiser, Corona, etc.) but there was one *big* surprise that was quite familiar to us: a Dogfish 60 Minute IPA, shipped about 2,200 miles from Milton, Delaware. I ordered one, of course.

Just like us—a long way from home

We enjoyed a quiet and relaxed dinner at Romo's, where I had what was quite simply the best shredded beef chimichanga of my life (and I've had a *lot* of "chimi"). Ivelis told me later during the trip that she had "food envy" as she watched my admittedly *vast* enjoyment of my menu choice.

Outside Romo's in Holbrook

After dinner, we walked the half mile west back to the Wigwam and settled in for the night in our *very* distinctive quarters after I took just a few more pictures. The sleeping area inside our tepee was actually reasonably roomy and both of us slept quite well that night.

Night comes to the Wigwam in Holbrook

Road Trip Statistics

Miles travelled on our sixth Route 66 day: **346**
Total travel time: **8 days**
Total miles traveled to this point: **2,533**
Miles from home at the end of this leg (shortest reasonable route): **2,146**

Day 7: from Holbrook, AZ to Barstow, CA

The morning drive from Holbrook to Peach Springs

Another Long Day on the Road

Ivelis and I woke up, showered carefully in our tiny bathroom with notably angled walls, packed, and left the Wigwam motel in the fairly early morning, knowing that we had to make some notable time to get to Barstow, California by evening—especially because there is a lot to see on the way.

As we departed Holbrook, we drove west for a little over a mile along Hopi Drive before getting back on Interstate 40 (again unavoidable) for about ten miles. We exited in tiny Joseph City (population 1,400 or so) to make a stop at the **Jack Rabbit Trading Post**, which dates from 1948 and is famous for the slogan "If you haven't been to the Jack Rabbit, you haven't been to the Southwest."

When we traveled Route 66 ten and fifteen years ago, billboards for the Jack Rabbit were visible for more than a thousand miles before you actually got there, but those signs are now largely (perhaps completely) gone. There are still a couple of the billboards as you get *much* closer.

The Jack Rabbit trading post itself was actually much smaller than I had expected: I had thought that it would be something like the rather large and even more heavily advertised Wall Drug in South Dakota. Still—it was worth the stop and worth the pictures. We would likely have purchased something if they had been open; but it was still fairly early in the morning.

After our stop at the Jack Rabbit (another Route 66 first for us), we rejoined the interstate and headed another 12 miles toward Winslow. We exited onto Highway 87 South, turned right onto 3rd Street and headed for the center of town. About three miles further along, we took a left at North Kinsley Avenue.

Parking on a Corner in Winslow, Arizona

The small city of Winslow has leveraged their most famous mention—by the Eagles all the way back in 1972—to the absolute hilt. The visitor can stop (and of course we did) at **Standin' on the Corner Park** on the corner of North Kinsley Avenue and Second Street and take your picture right next to an appropriately and cleverly configured flatbed Ford with a painting in a store window so you can see the girl described in the song and a life-size statue of a man with a guitar. After our photo opportunity, we stopped for a morning snack at a McDonald's about a mile further along.

One of the few remaining Jack Rabbit billboards

— 43 —

Parked right behind a flatbed Ford in Winslow

As we left Winslow, we rejoined Interstate 40 and headed towards Flagstaff, almost exactly 50 miles to the west. About 30 miles down the road, we could see the fading remnants of the distinctive **Twin Arrows Trading Post** off to our left as we headed west—though, strangely, the arrows themselves (which are actually ornamented telephone poles) seem to have been repainted relative recently—some more unexplained maintenance on the Mother Road.

What's left of the Twin Arrows Trading Post

I'll admit that we drove right on by Winona on this trip; one of our guidebooks writes "Winona kinda forgot itself"—a play on the "don't forget Winona" verse from Bobby Troup's (now there's a fellow with an *interesting* career) classic song "Route 66."

Flagstaff and Williams

On the other hand, Flagstaff today is a handsome and active city of about 69,000 with a distinct railroad influence. We exited the interstate and drove

> *A Short History of Our Cameras on Route 66*
>
> The first time the two of us drove Route 66 was all the way back in the analog camera days; do some of you even remember? Our "weapon of choice" in 2000 was a **Minolta Maxxum 5Xi** single lens reflex (SLR) camera, which turned out to be my final Maxxum and a camera that I *still* can't bring myself to get rid of, even though I haven't used it at all in several years.
>
> On our second Route 66 trip, I took my first digital SLR, a **Nikon D70**. This camera likely forever cemented my loyalty to Nikon as my digital SLR choice by *not* breaking when I clumsily and stupidly dropped it lens-first four feet onto concrete in downtown Chicago a couple of days into the trip. I sold this camera to a friend of mine (with full disclosure) several years ago. As of October 2015, she reports that it is still functional.
>
> On this time around, we were carrying a full frame **Nikon Df**—definitely *not* a shy and retiring camera, with its *very* retro looks and the large 24-120 zoom lens I paired with it. We were also in the process of learning how to use the camera; the *average* quality of the pictures we took definitely got steadily better as this trip progressed.

along the post-1947 route for almost five miles into downtown Flagstaff and its **Railroad Addition Historic District**, where we took a left onto Business Loop 40 and drove for about ten miles. As we exited Flagstaff we drove past the **US Naval Observatory**, which is the national dark-sky observing facility of the Department of Defense and home to a 61-inch telescope. Not content with being the location of one notable observatory, Flagstaff is also home to the circa 1894 **Lowell Observatory**, where Pluto was discovered in 1930.

Once again we rejoined Interstate 40 and headed past Bellemont for about 26 miles on our way towards Williams (the last town on all of Route 66 to be bypassed by the interstate—Williams held out until 1984). We exited onto Historic 66, drove

Entering Williams

through the center of town (passing the depot of the **Grand Canyon Railway**), and filled up at a Shell.

Some Great Driving in Arizona

From that point we headed about 22 miles along Interstate 40 until we passed Ash Fork (the "Flagstone Capital of the World") and exited at Crookton Road. We proceeded along Crookton Road for about 16 miles toward Seligman. One wonderful and relatively new (at least to us) touch we saw in Arizona were the reproduction Burma Shave signs placed by the Yavapai County public works department that showed up at various points along the road—you can see one full sequence of one poem in the annotated bibliography at the end of this book.

Somewhere between Ash Fork and Seligman

When we arrived in downtown Seligman, we drove along the classic strip, including the circa 1953 **Delgadillo's Snow Cap Drive-In** on the left and the circa 1958 **Supai Motel** on the right. John Lasseter,

Supai Motel sign in Seligman

the writer and director of *Cars*, has stated several times that the Radiator Springs location in the movie was loosely based on Seligman.

The 83-mile drive from Seligman to Kingman is substantially separated from the interstate, almost completely unspoiled, and (natch!) wonderful driving. Ivelis knows that I *really* enjoy this kind of driving and makes sure that I'm at the wheel when it happens.

Louis burbled happily as I drove us along through Peach Springs (passing the **Peach Springs Trading Post**), Truxton (with the **Frontier Motel and Restaurant**), Crozier, Valentine, and Hackberry. Just after passing the **Hackberry General Store**, we turned southwest and headed toward the city of Kingman.

Frontier Motel and Restaurant in Truxton

A Beloved Diner in Kingman

Route 66 heads under Interstate 40 and takes the driver straight into downtown Kingman, where the route is named Andy Devine Avenue (the 20th century character actor with the distinctive voice grew

The afternoon drive from Peach Springs to Barstow

up in Kingman). A couple miles further along, we stopped for lunch at the wonderful and colorful **Mr. D'z Route 66 Diner**.

The diner was absolutely packed on this particular early Saturday afternoon, which might have normally discouraged us, especially with the knowledge that we had over 200 miles further to go. However, we knew that our meal at Mr. D'z would be *excellent*: we've been there twice before, including on our first Route 66 trip. Ivelis had their "Tex Mex Burger" with green chili and jack cheese, while I had the "Route 66 Bacon Cheese Burger" (which really needs no further description).

Exterior of Mr.D'z Route 66 Diner in Kingman

Before we left Kingman, I walked a couple of blocks to get more cash at a Wells Fargo ATM—we had burned through almost all of what we had taken with us at the beginning of the trip. While I was doing this, Ivelis posed *Louis* next to the huge and beautiful Atchison, Topeka and Santa Fe engine number **3759**, a Baldwin steam locomotive dating from 1928 that travelled over 2.5 million miles during its career and is on the National Register of Historic Places. You can see a picture that hints at the locomotive's considerable scale in this book's credits section.

Serious Twisties Along the Sitgreaves Pass

As we left really interesting downtown Kingman (I'd like to spend some more time there), we headed southwest along Old 66 through Cool Springs and toward the famous **Sitgreaves Pass**. What had been a fairly straight road turned into a *very* windy and twisty one as we began to scale the Black Mountains, experiencing some quite sharp and tight hairpins on the way; terrain that was quite challenging for early travellers of Route 66. I absolutely *love* this driving—I feel that is what our Corvettes were designed for.

As we began to descend from the pass, we passed through the former mining town of Oatman—now a successful tourist attraction. While passing the historic **Durlin Hotel** (still open but no longer offering overnight accommodations) in the center of town, I drove very slowly and carefully to avoid hitting either the considerable weekend crowds of people or the famous burros (who are frightened of very little). Afterwards, Ivelis and I continued almost due south, driving another 26 miles through the

Just a few of the twisties in Sitgreaves Pass

glamorously named subdivision of Golden Shores before rejoining Interstate 40 in Topock.

… And Here We Are in California

Next, we crossed the Colorado River into California along Interstate 40—all the older bridges are gone. Shortly thereafter, we stopped and made absolutely sure that *Louis'* gas tank was completely full at a Mobil station in Needles (a small city named after a range of mountains to the south) before rejoining Interstate 40 and heading west into the Mojave Desert.

One area where Route 66 itself has *substantially* degraded since our last visit ten years ago was in eastern California. In the middle of what has mostly been a massive drought, heavy rains in September 2014 washed out more than *forty* bridges and a good portion of the roadbed between Goffs and Chambless.

Because of this relatively recent damage, we weren't able to leave Interstate 40 in California until we reached the Kelbaker Road exit; about 75 miles from the border. This unanticipated detour added a full 60 miles to our mileage for the day, making this by far our longest day on the Mother Road—but also a day with far more time spent away from it than we had expected.

Some Route 66 Sites Saved and Some Fading Away

Now **notably** off our planned course, we headed almost due south on the lonely and somewhat desolate Kelbaker Road for almost 12 miles. After finally getting back on Route 66 (often marked as the National Trails Highway in California), we doubled back east for about four miles on some of those *seriously* sketchy roads (Ivelis repeatedly asked if I thought we should turn around) to check on the state of the **Roadrunner's Retreat** in the ghost town of Chambless.

The news here for folks who either remember or have heard about the glory days of the Roadrunner's Retreat is *not* at all good. Though a chain link fence continues to at least somewhat protect the property, the buildings and sign all continue to disintegrate, about 20 years after the business finally closed. Ivelis stayed in the driver's seat with the engine running (I really couldn't blame her) while I took a few quick pictures.

The Roadrunner's Retreat fades away in Chambless

Ivelis made a quick but careful U-turn on the notably broken pavement and headed west along Route 66 for almost ten miles. In contrast to the Roadrunner's Retreat (which I don't expect to exist *at all* if/when we next travel Route 66), **Roy's Motel and Cafe** (this book's cover photograph) in Amboy is still very much a going concern, though it does seem that it is really just for Route 66 crazies like Ivelis and me at this point, along with (of course) the occasional movie or commercial. Some of the signage is in notably better shape than it was in 2005 and portions of Roy's are now actually open—a notable and positive change.

A motel front desk sits frozen in time at Roy's in Amboy

Bagdad and All That

After our happy and rather encouraging stop at Roy's, Ivelis and I headed northwest along Old 66 for almost 30 miles, driving past the theoretical *Bagdad Cafe* movie location (what little was left of the town after decades of decline was finally razed in 1991) on our way to Ludlow, where we rejoined Interstate 40.

About a century ago, Bagdad set a record for being the driest spot in the United States—from October 3rd, 1912 to November 8th, 1914, *no* rain fell for *767* days. 27 miles further west, we exited the interstate a little east of Newberry Springs (where much of *Bagdad Cafe* was actually shot in the mid-1980s).

We rejoined the National Trails Highway for about 16 miles through Daggett (home of the circa 1875 **Stone Hotel**). Fairly recent security concerns around the Marine Corps Logistics base located just to the east of Barstow forced us back on Interstate 40. Four miles down the road, we exited onto Main Street in Barstow and drove a little over two more miles to our stop for the night.

A Quiet Night in Barstow

Both of us were feeling rather tired when we pulled into the **Route 66 Motel** in the late afternoon. Built in 1922, the Route 66 Motel is both the oldest motel in Barstow and the oldest motel we stayed in on this trip. After checking in with the attentive and personable attendant, I parked *Louis* in front of our room and a Nash Metropolitan from the mid to late 1950s—a car shorter than a modern Mini.

For dinner, we walked about a quarter of a mile

Louis visits with a Nash Metropolitan in Barstow

west to **Rosita's**, where Ivelis had some *really* good margaritas. After our meal, the two of us walked slowly back east to our motel, where I took some more pictures and talked with a fellow Route 66 traveler in a sharp black Dodge Charger as night began to fall. After watching just a little bit of television, we both quickly fell into an exhausted sleep on one of the motel's distinctive round beds.

Route 66 Motel sign in Barstow

Road Trip Statistics

Miles traveled on our seventh Route 66 day: **520** (!)
Total travel time: **9 days**
Total miles traveled to this point: **3,053**
Miles from home at the end of this leg (shortest reasonable route): **2,587**

Day 8: from Barstow, CA to Santa Monica, CA

Beginning Our Final Day on Route 66

After waking, showering, dressing, and packing, we left our historic motel in Barstow in the early morning of a typically sunny and beautiful California Sunday. We departed Barstow along Main Street and headed about 36 quiet and scenic miles along the National Trails Highway through Lenwood, Hodge, Helendale, Oro Grande, and into the city of Victorville (population 121,000). Just after passing the not yet open for the day **California Route 66 Museum**, we turned right at 7th Street and headed towards the Interstate 15 on-ramp.

At about 9:00 AM and only a couple of a hundred feet before getting on the "superslab," we stopped for breakfast at **Richie's Real American Diner** just before the on-ramp and had our final great and filling diner breakfast of our trip. As we were paying our bill, one of the folks working there told us that we should come back soon. I responded as to how that was somewhat unlikely as we are from just outside of Philadelphia—it turned out that he thought we were from right "down the hill"; about 40 miles away in San Bernardino.

Booth at our diner in Victorville

After Victorville, there's really no option to get even reasonably quickly to the ocean shore but to take Interstate 15. One drives rapidly and *sharply* downhill (1,160 feet in five miles with a maximum grade of 6%) past Cajon Summit and Cajon Junction towards

Heading along the National Trails Highway

San Bernardino.

We ran into major construction (the three year, 325 million dollar "Devore Interchange Project") that rendered our Route 66-specific directions *completely* useless as we rapidly careered towards San Bernardino. Suddenly, we were more significantly off our planned route than at almost any other time on this particular Route 66 trip.

Magic Lamp Inn in Rancho Cucamonga

Major construction as we head towards San Bernardino

Luckily, some wasted time wasn't a major issue for us on this specific day. As Ivelis drove along, I quickly consulted our multiple analog and digital maps and came up with a reasonable solution. We ended up joining Interstate 210 north of Fontana, doubling back a few miles towards San Bernardino and successfully rejoining old 66 on Foothill Boulevard in the city of Rialto, where we passed a sister **Wigwam Motel** to the one in Holbrook.

Driving Slow Miles to the Coast

The extra time that we had allotted for this particular run at Route 66 and the fact that it was a Sunday in April allowed us to commit to taking almost all of the "correct" route through greater Los Angeles to the coast (instead of *hoping* to get there faster on the various interstates).

At about 10:40 AM, we filled up *Louis* at a Shell near Cypress Avenue in Fontana and began our run to the coast. Next on the route was Rancho Cucamonga, home of both the circa 1848 **Sycamore Inn** and the circa 1955 **Magic Lamp Inn** (with a lamp that lights with a gas flame in the evening). In often-busy suburban traffic, we followed Foothill Boulevard from Rancho Cucamonga through Upland, Claremont, La Verne, San Dimas, Glendora, and Azusa, where we stopped at a Starbucks for some refreshment.

Next came the tiny city of Irwindale (home of the once famous Irwindale Speedway—now marked for demolition), where Foothill Boulevard becomes Huntington Drive through Duarte and than turns back into Foothill Boulevard in about a mile and a half— we were a little confused but kept going.

We traveled a little over two miles on Foothill Boulevard in Monrovia before taking a left onto Santa Anita Avenue, a right onto Colorado Boulevard, and joining Colorado Street that becomes Colorado Boulevard after a couple miles (got that?).

Somewhere along this part of the route, we stopped at a coin-operated car wash. Ivelis turned out to have vastly more experience than I do with these contraptions, so she washed the car while I stayed out of the way, admired her handiwork (what had been a very dirty *Louis* soon looked more than respectable), and took a few pictures.

Heading Down the Arroyo Seco

Ivelis and I drove through downtown Pasadena before taking a left on South Arroyo Parkway. A little over a mile later, a signed welcomed us as we joined the **Arroyo Seco Parkway** itself. Crazily historic (it is on the National Register of Historic Places), the Arroyo Seco was the first freeway built in the western United States—it was completed in 1940.

Of course, the Arroyo Seco is now quite outdated after 75 years; the parkway was designed for 45 mph

When highways were considered postcard material

The Hollywood sign off in the distance

speeds and with 5 mph exits and *nobody* nowadays is travelling at those restrained speeds. We drove about nine nervous but still quite scenic miles (the northbound route is actually considered to be more scenic) before exiting onto the famous Sunset Boulevard in the Angelino Heights area of Los Angeles.

A classic Mustang on Sunset Boulevard

We headed northwest in dense but surprisingly polite traffic—I'm betting many folks driving behind *Louis* saw our Pennsylvania license plate and figured we were likely to be at least somewhat confused—along Sunset Boulevard for about three miles before successfully taking a somewhat challenging left onto Santa Monica Boulevard.

As we travelled slowly due west from West Hollywood to Beverly Hills, we could see the famous Hollywood sign looming about four miles off to our right.

At about 2:00 PM, we made our final stop before the end of our Route 66 trip. Hilariously (at least to me), it was at a McDonald's on Santa Monica Boulevard to a) use their rest rooms and b) get one more of their chocolate chip frappes.

After about twenty miles of driving west along the Santa Monica Boulevard, we began to see the Pacific Ocean in the distance. Old Route 66 actually didn't end at the **Santa Monica Pier**—it officially ended at the corner of Lincoln Boulevard and Olympic Drive. However, finishing a westbound trip at the pier is definitely more satisfying and that is what we chose to do.

We Make It to the Finish—Again

At 2:40 PM, we drove up onto the **Santa Monica Pier**, parked, and got out of the car—it had taken us about four hours to travel the last seventy miles from Rialto; far from our quickest pace. Ivelis and I find that there's always a "we actually made it" moment of celebration and relief at the end of one of our "big trips". So, we hugged, kissed, and took a few pictures of *Louis*, finally at rest after eight days on Route 66 and ten days from our house.

Next, we walked over to **66 to Cali** kiosk that was started by Dan Rice when he realized that was no real marker of the western end of Route 66. At the kiosk, we met Ian Bowen, who is Vice President West of the California Historic Route 66 Association. Ian filled us in on the history of the kiosk itself, as we stood smiling and very happy in the bright California sunlight.

Finally, Ivelis and I walked out to the very end of the pier, took a few a more pictures, and drank in the sense of being right on the Pacific Ocean after 2,394 miles on Route 66.

Louis, safely parked on the Santa Monica Pier

Road Trip Statistics

Miles traveled on our eighth and final Route 66 day: **134**

Total travel time: **10 days**

Total miles traveled to this point: **3,187**

Miles from home at the end of this leg (shortest reasonable route): **2,715**

The Return: from Santa Monica, CA to Bryn Mawr, PA

A Night Aboard the Queen Mary

After spending a few hours on the Santa Monica pier, we paid our parking exit fee and drove about thirty miles southeast to Long Beach for a night aboard the **Queen Mary** ocean liner, which was retired in 1967 and has been a hotel since 1972. So, after staying at many old hotels and old motels during most of our trip, we stayed in an old ocean liner for the big finish.

We drove east on Interstate 10 and then southeast on Interstate 405 before joining Interstate 710 and heading due south through some fairly extensive construction. We pulled up to the lovely Queen Mary and checked into our palatial room in the hotel— in Room 122 on Deck M (Main Deck) what had once been a first class cabin when the ship was still doing the transatlantic run. Afterwards we walked the decks of the Queen Mary, took a lot of pictures, and bought a souvenir or two.

Dinner that evening was at the Queen Mary's **Sir Winston's Restaurant and Lounge**, which advertises itself as "contemporary American." It is not (both the food and ambiance are quite traditional) but that doesn't matter—when one considers its *incredible* views, the food and drink is *way* better than it needs to be. We happily took advantage of the Caesar Salad for two prepared tableside.

After dinner, we headed to the ship's magnificent **Observation Bar and Art Deco Lounge** (what was the First Class Lounge in the Queen's sailing days)

Absolutely stunning Observation Bar on the Queen Mary

and likely had a few too many really good drinks in our highly celebratory mood. We also had a great time talking with Guillaume, a friendly and funny gentleman visiting from Canada.

In the morning, we woke up in our lovely room on the Queen Mary. We showered and dressed and I went outside for a couple minutes to take a few more photographs.

Queen Mary and Russian submarine in the early morning

Afterwards, we had a tasty breakfast at the Queen Mary's **Promenade Café** with our longtime Corvette friend Andy Bogus (yes, that's his real name) who lives in the nearby city of Torrance. Among other things, Andy is currently the owner of the Corvette Guru web site.

Turning Back East

The way back east following an east to west Route 66 trip has always been both anti-climatic and (by necessity) quick for us, but I did try to give this one some interest. Leaving Los Angeles on Monday morning turned out to be challenging, but not crazy. Doing exactly what Tammy the TomTom said, we drove on Interstate 710 to Interstate 105 to Interstate 605. Near Duarte, we turned due east onto Interstate 205, driving along it for about 19 miles before joining Interstate 15.

In the middle of the Mojave Desert, we filled up at Chevron in Baker. As we left town, Ivelis remembered that Baker is known for being the location of the world's tallest thermometer—something that would have fit in perfectly back when we were on Route 66. Despite the lack of early warning, I still managed to get a couple of pictures. We continued along Interstate 15 and crossed into Nevada near Primm, rapidly closing in on Las Vegas.

Before this trip, Ivelis had never been to an **In-N-Out Burger**. I finally got her to one on Blue Diamond Road in Las Vegas. She pronounced herself extremely happy with the burger but was not as impressed with the fries—something that turns out to be a not uncommon opinion.

World's tallest thermometer in Baker

Classically simple menu at In-N-Out Burger

One of the Seven Wonders of the Industrial World

After our quick lunch, we headed towards the **Hoover Dam**, which has been on Ivelis' "bucket list" for many years. It absolutely did not disappoint either of us. After parking above the Hoover Dam store on the west side, we walked across the top of the dam on

Looking south from the Hoover Dam

the south side, make sure to take many photographs along the way. We crossed back on the north side, taking note of how very low the water level is in Lake Mead. There are some "must-sees" for tourists that are quite simply just that, and the Hoover Dam is one of them.

Our Las Vegas stop was in **The Mirage**, which we had picked because we wanted to see the show located in the same casino with a minimum of fuss and movement once we arrived. Ivelis and I checked in to our rather nice room, unpacked, and changed. After going downstairs for a drink at the busy **Revolution Lounge**, we headed for our show, which was the Cirque du Soleil's **Love**, cleverly and enjoyably built around various songs by The Beatles.

After the very engaging and impressive show, we had a late dinner at **Tom Colicchio's Heritage Steak**, one last drink at their bar, and took the elevator up to our room on the 24th floor where we turned in for the night.

Serious Weather and Crazy Beauty in Utah

Quite early on the following morning, we left The Mirage in Las Vegas and headed for Denver—a *non-trivial* drive of a little over 750 miles. We joined Interstate 15 heading north at Flamingo Road in Las Vegas and crossed over into Arizona just after passing through Mesquite. Only 29 miles later, we were in Utah. Shortly before 10:00 AM, we stopped for a quick morning snack at a McDonald's in St. George before rejoining Interstate 15.

Later in the morning, we saw the most serious weather of this entire trip. There were warnings of high winds, which, in the arid west, were sure to bring dust storms. Sure enough, shortly after we made our big right hand turn at the intersection of Interstate 15 and Interstate 70, we ran into *non-trivial* dust storms, with visibility dropping down to about one eighth of a mile for us and the tractor trailers that seemed to be the only vehicles nearby.

As we headed east along Interstate 70 and began to climb in altitude, the dust storms faded away, though the wind (that constant wind) continued to make its presence felt. We stopped at some absolutely stunning

Dust storms along Interstate 70 in Utah

overlooks in Utah, including the Early Castle Valley stop in Emory.

Wow … Early Castle Valley overlook in Emory, Utah

Ivelis and I crossed into Colorado about 11 miles west of Mack and sped along through Glenwood Springs, Vail, and Silverthorne. After passing through the Eisenhower-Johnson Memorial tunnel, we began to descend towards Denver and civilization in the late afternoon.

Wonderful Denver

In Denver, we changed it up a little bit from our usual lodging choices and stayed at **the Curtis**, a Doubletree hotel with a strong pop culture theme. Our particular room was on the "big hair floor", so every time we arrived there, Marge Simpson greeted us and we walked by pictures of Poison and other eighties "hair bands" on the way to our room.

Our dinner that evening was at the superlative **Elway's Downtown** steakhouse in the Ritz-Carlton Hotel on Curtis Street, which I'm not ashamed to say that I've visited the last three times I've been in Denver. Elway's is absolutely *nothing* like the normal restaurant or sports bar that you might expect from a retired NFL quarterback. Once again, I enjoyed their spectacular looking and incredibly tasty shrimp cocktail while Ivelis raved about their filet mignon.

After finishing at Elway's, we headed back to our hotel, stopping for a nightcap at the cleverly named **Corner Office** bar before turning in for the night, exhausted after what had been our single longest driving day of this trip.

The next morning, we woke, showered, dressed, and went down to the Starbucks adjoining the hotel for a quick and at least somewhat healthy breakfast (I had the blueberry oatmeal) on a chilly and sunny morning—I've seen a bunch of those in Denver. Afterwards, we checked out of our hotel and headed east, taking Curtis Street, Martin Luther King Jr Boulevard, and Central Park Boulevard until we rejoined Interstate 70 at exit 279B.

About 15 miles further along the interstate, we filled up at a Shell in Watkins before traveling another 155 miles to the Kansas border.

Straight Across Kansas

About eight miles after crossing the border, we stopped at the *very* hospitable Kansas Travel Information Center in Goodland. In addition to having nice people, free coffee, and a place where you could pose with characters from the Wizard of Oz, the center also offers packets of sunflower seeds for the taking in appropriately labeled packages. The only thing that prevented Ivelis from grabbing some was her strong belief that she wouldn't be able to grow them on our fairly shady property back in Pennsylvania.

150 miles further east in Hays, we fueled at a Phillips 66 before stopping for lunch and some coffee. After our stop in Hays, we continued along Interstate 70 toward Kansas City.

Back in Kansas City

In Kansas City, we stayed for a second time at the **Westin Kansas City at Crown Center**, which is extremely well located—adjacent to the striking and impressive **National World War I Museum and Memorial** and not far from the gorgeous **Union Station**, built in 1914.

Liberty Memorial Tower lit up as night falls in Kansas City

For our dinner that evening, we walked just a few blocks to another one of our favorites from a previous trip; **Fiorella's Jack Stack Barbecue** in the Freight House. Ivelis had the amazing "Pork Rib Dinner" (four center-slab premium ribs) and I had the ridiculous "Jack's Best" sampler (one "Crown" prime beef rib, pork baby back ribs, and beef burnt ends).

Absolutely and completely stuffed, we walked the scenic but short route back to our hotel, stopping at **The Brasserie** for a quiet final drink before heading upstairs to our room.

Sunflower seeds available for the taking in Kansas

More Than Halfway Home

The next morning we called down to the valet desk to have *Louis* readied. When we got downstairs to pick up our car, one of the valets at the Westin recognized us from the year before, when we had passed through Kansas City in another Corvette that is notably older (more than a quarter of a century) than *Louis*. My experience continues to be that just when you don't expect folks to remember you (how many different cars does a valet see in a year?) is when they actually do.

Once again, we rejoined Interstate 70 and headed due east. We stopped for breakfast at a McDonald's in Columbia, Missouri. Afterwards, we filled up at a Mobil right down the road before head towards the St. Louis metropolitan area.

Ivelis and I re-crossed the Mississippi River on the quite new and rather gorgeous **Stan Musial Veterans Memorial Bridge**, which is known to locals as the "Stan Span".

Re-crossing the Mississippi River on Interstate 70

Shortly after crossing the Mississippi, we picked up Interstate 64. In Caseyville, Illinois we stopped shortly after noon to get a chocolate frappe to share. Next, we headed towards Louisville before turning northeast along Interstate 71 towards Cincinnati. In Corydon, Indiana we filled *Louis* up with premium at a Shell. Shortly afterwards, we ran into heavy rain as we neared Cincinnati.

In Cincinnati (a city neither of us had been to before), we stayed at the **Hilton Netherland Plaza**, a lovely old (circa 1931) art deco hotel with an interesting history, wonderful public spaces, nice rooms, and very hospitable service. We went to **Celestial Steakhouse** for dinner—as you'd expect from the name, it had a great view; ours looked down towards the center of the city and the Ohio River. Afterward we repaired to the spectacular **The Bar at Palm Court** in our hotel.

The Bar at Palm Court at our hotel in Cincinnati

Smooth Progress on Our Last Day Out

Early the next morning, we checked out of our gorgeous hotel and departed Cincinnati, knowing that it might be a long day but, barring major mechanical failure (unlikely in *Louis*), we would be home some time in the evening of the same day.

We rejoined Interstate 71 and stayed on it until we met up with Interstate 70 again near Columbus. From that point we passed quickly through West Virginia, entered Pennsylvania, and joined the Pennsylvania Turnpike in New Stanton.

After a rather surprisingly calm drive along the turnpike, we arrived back home at 6:20 PM on Friday,

Entering West Virginia on Interstate 70

April 17th, 2015. Ivelis and I had been on the road for 15 **full** days and had traveled 6,094 miles—an average of 406 miles per day; actually the *slowest* of our transcontinental trips in our *fastest* car. We had also gotten an average of 26.3 mpg over the entire trip—not at all bad for a fairly large high performance V8 being driven with little restraint.

Road Trip Statistics

    Days travel time for return: **5**
    Miles traveled on this leg: **2,907**
    Total travel time: **15 days**
    Total miles traveled for the entire trip: **6,094**

Afterword: Thoughts on What Route 66 Means in 2015

Route 66 is 89 years old.

I thought a lot during this trip about why Ivelis and I keep coming back to it. It certainly isn't convenient—staging to it takes two days. It also isn't in either of our family's heritage—I can't find anybody from either side who ever traveled Route 66 before it was officially decertified in 1985. The author of this book's foreword, Jim O'Donnell, *definitely* has much more of a familial connection to the Mother Road.

Route 66 is, I think, emblematic of an idea for the two of us and, I know, many others: the great open American road. There are many others—the Lincoln Highway, which we traveled in 2014, comes quickly to mind—but they're not quite the same. Route 66 is also, of course, the name of that seminal television show which ran from 1960 to 1964; and a reason that driving the route in a Corvette always make sense.

Of course, all is not well. We're still losing sites and places to stay along the route—the Gardenway Motel closed early in 2015. Some sites that were merely closed ten years ago are nearing ruins status now.

I was also very conscious on this trip of the disappearance of the road itself. In particular, I have little hope that the Ribbon Road in eastern Oklahoma will be around for many more years. The roads in the Mojave Desert in eastern California that were sketchy but passable in 2005 are completely off-limits to normal cars in 2015, and there are *so many* routes where the only option if you don't have a 4x4 and/or special permission is to get on the interstate.

There are also changes in the very act of driving an automobile itself. I remember writing a "think piece" back in 1993 postulating that my friends thought I was weird because I still drove my own car, but that world is now fast approaching. For all of the technology present in Ivelis' magnificent 2012 Corvette, I see it as becoming very "old school" in a relatively short amount of time.

Finally, I fear that what will end up happening to Route 66 will be somewhat like what has happened to antique cars—the only ones left are the nice or special ones, so one loses touch with the overall experience of how they really were back when they were just cars. In ten more years, will we be able to drive Route 66 as just a road?

Portion of Route 66 passable in 2005 but not in 2015

Lists

Music

In contrast to previous "big trips," we didn't make a big deal about the music we were bringing with us on this particular "gallivant." I think part of the reason is that high quality audio is so easy now: our iPhones effortlessly hook up to the nine-speaker car stereo (I know—we're lucky) and, if we get bored with what we have with us, we can always revert to our Sirius/XM satellite radio.

Equipment and Tools in the Car

Halon fire extinguisher
Combination battery charger and tire inflater
Mobil 1 synthetic oil (one quart) and some oil rags
Three different multi-tools
First aid kit
Griot's Garage car cleaning supplies
And, watching over us, because it is *always* good to have professionals available: AAA Plus and Hagerty High-Octane.

Things We Think We Missed

If we ever do travel Route 66 again, we'd like to give Oklahoma City, McLean, Amarillo, and Albuquerque some more time, instead of driving right on by. We'd also like to explore *more* of Pontiac (there's a ton of stuff we missed while we were busy getting lost), Tulsa, Gallup, Kingman, Needles, and San Bernadino (darn construction!).

Post Script: What's Happened Since the Trip

Our Michelin Pilot Sport all-season tires gave their all on this trip. When we switched to our summer tires shortly after returning home, all four of the tires coming off showed damage, including significant cracks. They were, of course, replaced—you don't mess with tires.

Louis turned over 40,000 miles on a much shorter three-day trip in late August.

And, of course, we began planning for another long trip in a Corvette with in the next few years …

Blues Brothers forever dancing in Joliet, Illinois

Annotated Bibliography

Antonick, Mike. *Corvette Black Book 1953-2013*. Mount Vernon, OH: Michael Bruce, 2012.

The absolutely essential pocket Corvette reference, the *Corvette Black Book* will keep you from looking like a complete fool at almost any Corvette gathering, no matter what part of this vast hobby you are involved in. Antonick revises and updates the *Black Book* every year (he's been at it since 1978), but mine (and it is definitely not my first) is now a couple of years old—stained with dirt, brake fluid, and motor oil and full of notes and extra statistics. *You* should definitely get the latest and greatest version.

Knowles, Drew. *Route 66 Adventure Handbook, Fourth Edition*. 2011.

Knowles takes a different approach here—this exhaustive book is his view of things you should know as you travel along. Every town (and ghost town) is at least listed and his context is often interesting and useful. A good complement to McClanahan's *EZ66 Guide*—what? You thought you could travel Route 66 with just one book?

McClanahan, Jerry. *The EZ66 Guide For Travelers, Third Edition*. 2014.

This spiral bound book is not optional—at least if you want to miss the minimum number of turns (*nobody* actually trying to travel the Mother Road misses zero turns). I hope Jerry keeps updating this guide—he's been at it for ten years now and I think it's a huge success.

Moore, Bob and Grauweis, Patrick. *Route 66. The Illustrated Guidebook To The Mother Road*. Williams, AZ: Roadbook, 1998.

Now a little dated (we got our copy used), but beautifully laid out—a really great way to start figuring out the sights you might want to see on Route 66.

National Historic Route 66 Federation. *Route 66 Dining & Lodging Guide - 17th Edition*. 2015.

Great and up-to-date advice on where to eat and stay on Route 66 (we actually travelled with the 16th edition which has since revised), crowd-sourced from National Historic Route 66 Federation members. We found many of our best food experiences on this trip in this guide—without it, we might have missed the Old Route 66 Family Restaurant, Granny Shaffer's, and the Range Café.

Wallis, Suzanne Fitzgerald and Wallis, Michael. *The Art Of Cars*. San Francisco, CA: Chronicle, 2006.

Sometimes mass-market merchandising produces beautiful things almost in spite of itself, and this book describing and showing how the *Cars* movie was visualized and designed is just such a case.

Replica Burma Shave signs in Arizona

Index

A

Afton 23
   Rest Haven Motel 23
Albuquerque 38
   KiMo Theater 38
Amarillo 29
   Cadillac Ranch 29
Amboy 48
   Roy's Motel and Cafe 48
Arcadia 26
   round barn 26
Arizona 40–42
Arroyo Seco Parkway 52
Atlanta 10
   Downey Building 10
Automotive News 31

B

Barstow 48–49, 51
   Rosita's 49
   Route 66 Motel 48
Baxter Springs 22
   Phillips 66 Station 22
Bernallilo 37
   Range Café 37
Bogus, Andy 55
Braidwood 7
   Polk-a-Dot Drive In 7
Burma Shave 45

C

Cadillac 4, 38
California ix, 47–48, 51–55
Cars movie 21, 45
Carthage 20
   G&E Tire Company 20
Catoosa 23
   Blue Whale of Catoosa 23
Chambless 47
   Roadrunner's Retreat 47
Chevrolet, Louis xi
Chicago 3–5
   David Burke's Prime House 4
   Grant Park 4
   MV Abegweit 4
   The Congress Plaza Hotel 4–5
Clinton 27
   Oklahoma Route 66 Museum 27
Colorado 57–58
Continental Divide 39
Cuba 14

D

Dodge Charger sedan 49
Dodge Monaco sedan 6
Dogfish 60 Minute IPA 42
Doolittle, Jimmy 15
Dwight 7
   Ambler's Texaco gas station 7
   Old Route 66 Family Restaurant 7

E

Elway's Downtown 58
Elwood 6
   Abraham Lincoln National Cemetery 6

F

Fanning 14
   Fanning 66 Outpost and General Store 14
   world's largest rocking chair 14
Ferrari 250 GT 31
Fiorella's Jack Stack Barbecue 58
Flagstaff 44
Ford Mustang coupe 53
Ford pickup truck 34

G

Galena 20
   Cars On The Route 21
Gallup 39–40
   El Rancho Hotel & Motel 39
General Motors Heritage Center xi
Grapes of Wrath, The ix, 33
Gray Summit 13
   Gardenway Motel 14

Groom 28
   leaning water tower 28
Guinness Book of World Records 14

H

Hilton Netherland Plaza 59
Holbrook 41–43
   Romo's restaurant 42
   Wigwam Motel 41–43
Hooker Cut 15
Hoover Dam ix, 56

I

Illinois 3–4, 5–10, 59
Indiana 3, 59
In-N-Out Burger 56

J

Joliet 6
   Dick's Towing 6
   Rich & Creamy 6, 63
   Route 66 Food N Fuel 6
Joplin 20
   Granny Shaffer's Family Restaurant 20
Joseph City 43
   Jack Rabbit Trading Post 43

K

Kansas 20–22, 58–59
Kingman 45–46
   Atchison, Topeka & Santa Fe steam engine 46, 73
   Mr. D'z Route 66 Diner 46
Kirk, Dessa 4

L

Lasseter, John 45
Lincoln Continental Mark IV coupe 41
Lincoln Highway ix, 61
Lingenfelter Camaro coupe 41
Los Angeles 53
Los Lunas 38

M

Mantle, Mickey 22
Miami 22
   Waylan's Ku-Ku Burger 22
Michaels, Al xiv
Missouri 10–11, 13–20, 59

Mojave Desert 47, 61

N

Nash Metropolitan coupe 48
National Corvette Museum xi–xiii
National Packard Museum 1–2
Needles 47
Nevada 56–57
New Mexico 29–31, 33–36
Normal 8

O

Oatman 46
Odell 8–9
   Standard Oil gas station 8–9
Ohio 1–3, 59
Oklahoma 22–27
Oklahoma City 27

P

Packard Caribbean convertible 1–2
Painted Desert Inn 40
Paris Springs Junction 19
   Gay Parita Sinclair Station 19
Pecos 34
Pennsylvania 1, 59
Pennsylvania Turnpike ix, 1, 59
Petrified Forest National Park 40–41
Pontiac 8

Q

Queen Mary ocean liner 55

R

Rancho Cucamonga 52
   Magic Lamp Inn 52
Rialto 52
   Wigwam Motel 52
Ribbon Road 22–23
Riverton 21
   Marsh Rainbow Arch Bridge 21
Rolla 15
   Joe & Linda's Tater Patch 15
Roosevelt, Theodore 40

S

Saint Clair 14

San Bernardino 52
Santa Fe 35–37
  Back at the Ranch 35
  Eldorado Hotel 36
  El Rey Inn 37
  Geronimo restaurant 36
  Hilton Santa Fe Historic Plaza 35
  Santa Fe Plaza 35
  Thunderbird Bar & Grill 35
Santa Monica 53
  Santa Monica Pier 53
Santa Rosa 33–34
  Joseph's Bar & Grill 34
  Route 66 Auto Museum 34
Seligman
  Supai Motel 45
Sitgreaves Pass 46
Springfield, Illinois 10
  Illinois State Capital 10
Springfield, Missouri 15–19
  Flame steakhouse 17
  Rest Haven Court 16
  Route 66 Rail Haven motel 16–19
St. Louis 10–11, 13
  Coral Court motel 10–11
  Gateway Arch 13
Stroud 26
  Skyliner Motel 26

T

Texas 28–29
Texola 28
TireRack xiii, 3
Truxton 45
  Frontier Motel and Restaurant 45
Tucumcari 29–33
  Blue Swallow Motel 30–33
  Boulevard Cleaners and Laundromat 31
  Motel Safari 30
  Pony Soldier Motel 30
  Pow Wow Restaurant & Lizard Lounge 30
Tulsa 23–25
  Meadow Gold sign 25
  Meteor 4500 steam engine 25
  The Campbell Hotel 23–25

U

Utah 57

V

Victorville 51
  Richie's Real American Diner 51
Villa Ridge 14
  Sunset Motel 14
Virginian, The ix

W

Wayne, Anthony 15
Weatherford 27
  Stafford Air & Space Museum 27
Webb City 20
West Virginia 59
Wilmington 6–7
  Gemini Giant 6–7
Winona 44
Winslow 43
  Standin' on the Corner Park 43

X

Y

Z

Credits

All images (about 90) copyright © 2015 John Mulhern *unless* otherwise listed below

Images on pages 7 (Elvis), 8 (Palace of Sweets and road), 9, 14 (Sunset Motel and Mural), 15 (4-Lane 66), 16, 20 (G&E Tire building and entering Kansas), 22 (Ku-Ku burger), 23 (ribbon road and Rest Haven sign), 33 (road), 34, 35 (Pecos, pre-1937 route, and boots), 38 (KiMo Theater), 39 (Corvette/Cadillac and Los Alamitos sign), 41 (Painted Desert Inn), 45 (road, Supai Motel, and Frontier Motel), 47, 51 (towards bridge), 57 (dust storms), 59 (both bridges), 61, 63, and 66 (entire sequence) copyright © 2015 Ivelis Mulhern

All maps copyright © 2015 Map Resources, modified by John Mulhern III

Image on page ix courtesy of Jim O'Donnell

Centennial Corvette images on page xi © General Motors

Image outside the National Corvette Museum on page xii courtesy of the National Corvette Museum

TireRack logo on page xiii courtesy of TireRack

Overhead image of TireRack headquarters and distribution center on page 3 courtesy of TireRack

Postcard images on pages 3, 11, and 37 courtesy of the Tichnor Brothers Collection, Boston Public Library

Water tower image on page 14 courtesy of James Hayes, substantially cropped

Hotel image on page 35 © 2015 Hilton Hotels & Resorts

Postcard image on page 53 courtesy of the National Park Service

Elway's Downtown logo on page 58 courtesy of Elway's

Hotel bar image on page 59 © 2015 Hilton Hotels & Resorts

After serving as an avionics technician in the U.S. Navy, John Mulhern III attended Drexel University, receiving a BS in Information Systems with concentrations in artificial intelligence, database development, and human interface design.

John has worked at the University of Pennsylvania (alma mater of Bobby Troup) for over twenty-five years. He is currently Lead for Client Technologies, a role in which he has served since 2008 and in which he focuses on the future technology needs of everyone from incoming freshman students to emeritus faculty members.

John has published two books previously under the J3Studio Press imprint: *A 21st Century Road Trip*, which was published in 2006 and chronicles a 2005 trip on Route 66 and the Pacific Coast Highway in a 2003 Corvette convertible and *Lincoln Highway 101*, which was published in 2015 and details a rather fraught 2014 trip along the Lincoln Highway in a 1985 Corvette coupe.

John resides in Bryn Mawr, PA with his lovely wife Ivelis, and his beloved Corvettes: *Lauren*, *Grace*, and *Louis*.

Ivelis Mulhern attended Drexel University, receiving a BS in Business Administration with concentrations in accounting and finance. While at Drexel, she sang mezzo-soprano with multiple groups and played the female lead in *Man of La Mancha* during her senior year.

Ivelis is currently a Certified Financial Planner™ Practioner with Ameriprise Financial Services, Inc and has been with Ameriprise (and its predecessor American Express Financial Advisors) since 1996.

Ivelis resides in Bryn Mawr, PA with her husband John, who she has been married to for over twenty years.

Louis waits next to Santa Fe 3759 in Kingman, Arizona